PELICAN BOOKS

CHE'S GUERRILLA WAR

Régis Debray was born in 1941 and educated at the
École Normale Supérieure, where he studied with the
Marxist philosopher, Louis Althusser. When he first went
to Cuba in 1961 he observed the great literacy campaign
which resulted in Cuba's becoming the first Latin American country to wipe out illiteracy. Later he spent long
periods in South America, studying the various radical
parties and movements and visiting guerrilla fronts
where possible. On the basis of these experiences he
wrote two long articles, 'Le Castrisme: la longue marche
de l'Amérique Latine', published in Sartre's review,
Les Temps Modernes, in 1963, and 'América Latina: algu-
nos problemas de estrategia revolucionaria', in 1965;
these articles establi⬚⬚⬚⬚⬚

He returned to Cu⬚⬚⬚⬚
sophy at the Univer⬚⬚⬚⬚
to numerous unp⬚⬚⬚⬚
participants in the ⬚⬚⬚⬚
with Fidel Castro, ⬚⬚⬚⬚
Revolution in the Rev⬚⬚⬚⬚
Debray went to Bolivia as a correspondent of the
Mexican weekly *Sucesos* and the Paris publishing house
of Maspero, to report on the then newly opened guerrilla
fronts. He was arrested by the Bolivian police while
travelling under his own name and in civilian clothes.
He was charged with aiding the guerrilla insurrectionists
active in Bolivia, thought to have been led by Castro's
ex-aide and confidant, Ernesto 'Che' Guevara. Despite
pleas for clemency from many world figures Debray was
sentenced to thirty years' imprisonment, but was released
in 1970. *Revolution in the Revolution?* was published in
Penguins in 1968. *Prison Writings* is to be published by
Penguins in 1975.

RÉGIS DEBRAY

Che's Guerrilla War

Translated by
Rosemary Sheed

PENGUIN BOOKS

Penguin Books Ltd, Harmondsworth, Middlesex, England
Penguin Books Inc., 7110 Ambassador Road, Baltimore, Maryland 21207, U.S.A.
Penguin Books Australia Ltd, Ringwood, Victoria, Australia
Penguin Books Canada Ltd, 41 Steelcase Road West, Markham, Ontario, Canada
Penguin Books (N.Z.) Ltd, 182–190 Wairau Road, Auckland 10, New Zealand

—

La Guérilla du Che first published by Éditions du Seuil 1974
This translation first published 1975
Reprinted 1975

—

Copyright © Rosemary Sheed, 1975

—

Made and printed in Great Britain
by Hazell Watson & Viney Ltd,
Aylesbury, Bucks
Set in Monotype Baskerville

To the memory of Jose Cabrera Flores,
'El Negro',
Peruvian doctor and internationalist fighter
who loved his people, his work,
and the music of Mozart.

*

*Killed 2 September 1967,
near the village of Palmerito,
in south-east Bolivia.*

Contents

The generosity and active solidarity
of François Maspero
over the course of years
have made it possible for this book
to see the light of day.
I here offer him the homage
of faithful friendship.

Preface

'WE are dwarfs perching on the shoulders of giants. We can see better and further than they can – not because our sight is keener or our height greater, but because they are carrying us, raising us to their own gigantic level . . .'

I want to take these words – spoken by Bernard of Clairvaux some time around the year 1200 – at once as a text and as an excuse. When a giant dies, there will be plenty of hair-splitting, opinionated dwarfs to rush forward with rational explanations as to why, 'logically', that was how it was bound to end, and to pinpoint the 'mistakes' he made when he was alive. Little though we may like it, we must now become part of that valiant army of dwarfs and set about the unpleasant job of explaining the reasons for Comandante Guevara's military failure in Bolivia in 1967. At best this must be a distasteful undertaking, at worst something of a profanation. And readers will realize that this must be the case for me, of all people – for several reasons. My heart sinks at the thought of seeming to abandon all considerations of sentiment and loyalty; but Che's own writings, and the memory of his conversation, of his Leninist capacity for self-criticism – subjecting the progress of the revolution to the most merciless and objective judgement with a sarcasm which spared neither himself nor anyone else – will provide me with the necessary spur. A surgeon at the operating table has no friends, no feelings, no memories – only an operation to perform, the instruments to do it with, and a basic knowledge of anatomy and physiology. An analysis of this sort is not unlike a surgical operation; and no one knew this better than Che, who was constantly conducting the most painful operations on himself and on others.

True, the only people who can make an honest analysis

of the reasons for a temporary defeat are those who have emerged from it unharmed – and that is a distinction of which no one is proud. The perspicacity which makes survival possible is a gift most of us would rather be without. But in the circumstances, since with hindsight every individual moment can be seen as though by X-ray, it would be dishonourable to evade the responsibility that falls upon any intelligent agent of human history to reflect on the causes and conditions of the failure. Thus do we transform event into experience, and negative into positive, drawing from defeat that vital seed which, if properly sown and protected, can grow into a future victory. The international workers' movement, and the Marxist–Leninist theory which provides its 'guideline for action', has not as yet found any other way of progressing than by continuing indefatigably to re-examine the past.

For the dwarfs, with their reasoning and keen vision, have made great progress since the Middle Ages. The development of knowledge has given them the tools and scientific method they need to rationalize the untidiness of history and, after the event, to see things as necessary which were, at the time, only possible and contingent. We now have available to us a science that is still new and somewhat uncertain – historical materialism – whose cornerstones have been laid by Marx, Lenin and others, and which enables us to see the anatomy and physiology of social development a little more clearly. Now, we cannot for a moment forget

(a) that the dialectic of history would not be materialist if, as Marx reminded Kugelmann after the bloody failure of the Paris Commune, all the battles were won in advance, and every episode in the class struggle was assured of victory. In that case history would be 'something mystical', and there would ultimately be no point in fighting any battle – indeed there would be no one to fight it, since there would be no reason for fighting;

(b) that historical materialism would not be dialectical if

'error' were automatically the opposite of 'truth' – as though it were the negative of an external positive, whereas in fact the positive emerges from within the negative and develops actually through the working of the negative.

Only afterwards, only from a distance, does the confused muddle of impressions, expectations, surprises and interconnections which go to make up an 'event' combine into a rational, comprehensible whole which one can then try to break down into clear and distinct components. At the time, all the decisions, actions, options which may well be seen as so many 'inadequacies', 'incorrect estimates of the situation', 'ideological deviations', were mine. I took an active, though modest, part in them, and in areas where I did not take part directly or indirectly, whether from my own lack of knowledge or skill, or because of the compartmentalizing of functions essential in any clandestine operation, I fully believed them to be right. That is why I began with the twofold profession of faith and humility of St Bernard who was a monk and thus also, perhaps in spite of himself, a 'giver of lessons'. It is not just that I want it to be clear to those who consider my analysis a sound one that any discernment there may be is entirely retrospective and *a posteriori*; also, and above all, I want it to be clear to everyone that, in the rising spiral of social praxis and critical praxis, it is always the former that bears the major stress. Or, better perhaps: if there should arise any contradiction in the dialectical relationship of unity and difference existing between the critique of arms and the weapon of criticism, it is the critique of arms which constitutes the basic and pre-eminent aspect of the contradiction.

It is right to fight. It is right to discover the reasons for one's defeats. It is right to fight again, on the basis of the lessons gained from previous experience. And so on, indefinitely, indefatigably, to victory: *¡Hasta la victoria siempre!*

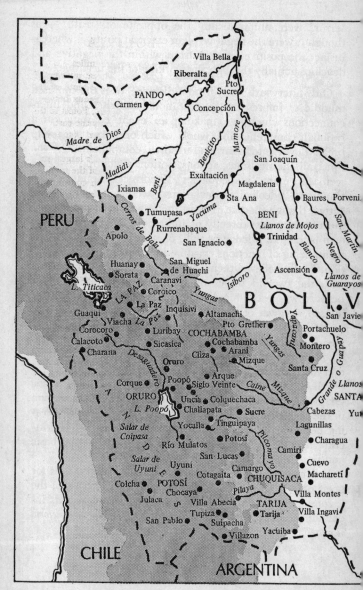

BOLIVIA

Land area: 415,000 square miles.

Population: 4,700,000. Three quarters of the population occupy one tenth of the land, mainly the high plateaux between Lake Titicaca to the north, Potosí to the south, and Cochabamba to the east.

Principal towns: La Paz (500,000), Cochabamba (100,000), Santa Cruz, Sucre. Bolivia is the world's largest producer of tin (14 per cent of the total, or about 25,000 tonnes of tin concentrates in 1968). There are also large iron mines (Mutún is the world's largest reserve), zinc, wolfram, copper, gold and silver.

The average per capita income is $158 per year (1968 estimate). The mortality rate is 23 per 1,000. There is one doctor for every 3,250 people (but no doctors in the country areas). Life expectancy is 48 years for men, 52 for women (and the average is much lower for miners).

In 1968, of the population of school age and older, 70 per cent were estimated to be illiterate.

There are 475 miles of asphalted roads; 2,200 miles of railways. Mining products accounted for 94 per cent of the export earnings in 1966 (83 per cent in 1968), though 48·7 per cent of the working population are employed in agriculture and stock-breeding (1965 figure).

BRAZIL

San Ignacio

I A

San Matías

San Miguel

Sta Rosa

anJosé
e Chiquitos

San Juan

Pto Quijarro

Chiquitos

Sto Corazón

RUZ

Robore

Sta Ana

Pto Suarez

PARAGUAY

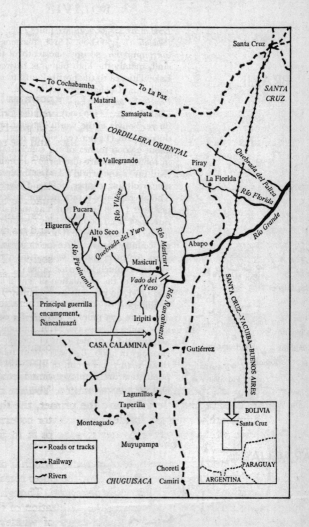

I

A Detonation without an Explosion, or an Instructive Massacre

ONE evening, in March 1967, in the camp known as 'El Oso', a discussion arose between a newly arrived Bolivian comrade and a Cuban comrade about the role of guerrilla warfare in the political situation of the country, and the role of the Cubans in guerrilla warfare. Che, who had just got back from a lengthy and exhausting exploration of the area between the *campamento central* and the Río Grande, called together the two centre and rearguard squads to talk to them. He began with the Bolivian comrades, explaining the point of the Cuban participation in general, and his own in particular, alongside them; then to everyone he explained the effect of guerrilla intervention on Bolivian society. The two explanations were similar. Che explained that he and his fellows had not come to fight *instead* of the people of Bolivia, but only to help them launch *their* war of liberation. Therefore, the Bolivians now involved in the guerrilla war must bear in mind that, once the period of education and training was over, the main burden and responsibility of leadership of their country would inevitably fall upon them. 'As for the rest of us,' he said, to illustrate his point further, 'our function is not even that of the detonator. You are the detonator. We are much less. We are the primer, the thin layer of fulminate of mercury inside the detonator covering the explosive which merely activates it – helps it to fire better. That's all.'

In copper detonators, fulminate of mercury, which is one of the 'originating' explosives, is laid over the outer surface of the 'bursting' explosive – tetryl or hexogene. Though it does not directly cause it, it ensures the detonation of the capsule, which in turn sets off the charges of whatever explosive the capsule has been put into.

What happened at Ñancahuazú? The fuse was lit. The capsule detonated and burst. But the general explosion did not take place at once. It happened later, like a time bomb, and the tremendous shock-waves have gone on widening year by year, shaking Bolivian society at every level, and beyond Bolivia, the whole of America. But at the time and place of setting it off, the *tactically* decisive time and place, nothing much happened. Why not?

To continue with Che's metaphor, in the short term, and with regard only to the technical aspect of the thing, the failure might have had two explanations:

– *the capsule may have been badly positioned:* the detonator was not in direct physical contact with a charge effective enough to produce the explosion. In the area of the guerrilla group's movements and operations (and later, after the separation from Joaquín,* of those of the two remaining columns), class conflicts were subordinate, diluted, incapable of receiving and transmitting any revolutionary message. Socially, historically and politically, that was not 'where the action was'. This brings us to the problem of selecting the guerrilla war zone, and the circumstances surrounding that selection – a practical problem, yes, but one which in turn depends on a far larger question which it inevitably poses: the class character of the peasants of the area, and their relationship with the moving forces of the Bolivian revolution;

– *perhaps there was no fuse to carry the flame along to the explosives:* if a guerrilla operation is not in direct contact with a socially favourable situation, if the really powerful social charge that is ready to explode is somewhere else – in the mines, in La Paz, in the proletariat and the politically aware urban bourgeoisie – then clearly there must be a definite link there, between the two, the detonator and the explosive, the vanguard and the moving forces of the revolution. That link is a system of communication and supplies – men, information, orders, arms and ammunition, food – operating in both directions between the guerrillas and the town centres. Such a system is both technical and

* See Chronology of Che in Bolivia, p. 153.

political since the technical operation – with contacts, couriers, reinforcements – is inseparable from its political content, and the importance it is given in the guerrillas' general scheme of things. In Bolivia in 1967 no such technical system had been established by the time military operations began, and the embryonic system which should have supplied for it was not in evidence at all. This brings us to the practical problem of the establishment and history of the *red urbana*, the urban network or rearguard. And this again depends on a more basic, political problem: is not some kind of political support, however rudimentary, a vital necessity if the guerrilla war is to develop? And given the methods used, was it possible to establish any political set-up? Could a rearguard with no specific political identity, and no possibility of forming alliances with nationally established popular forces, fulfil even the modest role of logistical support that was expected of it? And finally, given the peculiar nature of its class structure, its historical traditions of fighting and its recent political history, was it possible in Bolivia to relegate the urban centres and huge settlements of mineworkers to the role of a rearguard or a mainly logistical support force?

Before trying to answer these questions, or even see if they are the right questions to ask, let us continue to look directly at the situation as it appeared in 1967. The two elements I have mentioned – the sterility of the immediate area around the guerrilla headquarters, and the lack of any system of communication between the guerrillas and the social forces of the revolution – combined to make the small motor working at full capacity (the guerrilla war) out of phase with the large motor which was at that time barely ticking over (the national mass movement). So, though the small motor actually got the large motor going, the two remained running side by side without managing to connect at all. The small motor was therefore left to work as it were on a closed circuit, with only its own reserves of energy to call on; once those were exhausted, being unable to re-charge itself from outside or make contact with any of the possible sources of energy, it stopped. Those sources of energy, on the other hand, could not be properly motorized so as to transform their potential into any concretely effective political work, and they too used up all their reserves in a useless sacrifice. This is perhaps the best way to describe, in terms of the *foquista* metaphor of the two motors, the latent tragedy which came to the surface on 24 Jnue 1967, with the St John's Day massacre. The isolation of the guerrilla force from the other important centres in the country, the decisive social and political centres, had one immediate and peculiarly cruel effect: the evidence of active solidarity with the guerrilla fighters demonstrated by the tin miners, the real base of the proletariat, was of no use to those for whom it was actually intended.

For in fact, to return to our other metaphor, there was an explosion, produced perhaps by the detonation of the capsule, but not determined by it, in a place where an accumulated charge of class hatred and brutal exploitation had produced an atmosphere quite specially sensitive to any suggestion of revolution. The repercussions of the guerrilla war were thus quite remote from it geographically; the effect was out of all proportion to the cause and beyond its control; and though the guerrilla offensive produced an effect, it took the form of spontaneous and unilateral solidarity rather than a movement of aggressive protest actively harnessed to the guerrilla war.

In June, the FSTBM (Bolivian miners' union), which was then a clandestine operation, had convoked at Siglo Veinte, the centre of the mining area, an *ampliado minero* – a workers' congress enlarged to include industrial workers, and university students and teachers. Shortly before this, the Catavi mine section had adopted a resolution that the miners of that district would give a day's wages (out of their below-subsistance pay) and some medical supplies (of which they had all too few) to the guerrilla fighters of the south east. Simón Reyes, the union's *secretario de relaciones*, went from where he had been hiding in Oruro to Siglo

Veinte to organize and preside over this general assembly of workers which was to work out the ways and means for combined action in support of their demands. They had a real grievance in 1965, the Barrientos–Ovando military junta had reduced the wages of those working for Comibol (the nationalized Bolivian Mining Corporation) by 45 per cent at one blow – certainly a unique step in our time; for, though restrictions of purchasing power and wage freezes are familiar enough, a government decree reducing salaries by half from one day to the next is hardly a common event. The workers met inside the mine with their leaders, and the secret assembly, among other things, ratified the Catavi decision. Shortly after this, on 24 June, the army quietly arrived by train, encircled the mining encampments, and at dawn launched an out-and-out attack on what the High Command described as 'enemy territory'. The attack was particularly outrageous because it caught the miners while still asleep after the peaceful feast of St John when, on what is reputedly the coldest night of the *altiplano* winter, there are bonfires, dancing and drinking everywhere – a national ritual in fact. This attack was described by the government as 'preventive'; to justify themselves afterwards, they quite falsely accused the miners of intending to attack the Challapata garrison near Lake Poopó – a ludicrous suggestion since at that moment there was only one battalion of engineers there, and they had almost no weapons. The miners, at home and asleep in their beds, were in no state to defend themselves. However, the alarm siren sounded, and they fought valiantly with dynamite and a few antique Mauser rifles from the 1914 war. But resistance was useless. The number of deaths was given officially as thirty. In fact, almost seventy miners, and their wives and children, were killed, in their homes or in the streets of Siglo Veinte. This magnificent action by the armed forces now figures in the already plentiful history of Bolivian workers' martyrdom as 'the massacre of San Juan'.

The massacre was a twofold tragedy, both for what it was in itself, and for what it was *not* in relation to the guerrillas.

The isolation of the workers' sacrifice echoed the isolation of the guerrillas' sacrifice, like the obverse and reverse of the same coin, a double punishment meted out to a single failure. As the crow flies, it is barely 160 miles across the central Andes from Uncía to Vallegrande, yet the miners and the guerrillas watched without actually seeing each other, like beings from two different worlds. Objectively they needed each other. Neither guerrillas nor miners could achieve their individual aims without the others' help. If they were not to die of hunger, or be killed by bullets, the miners needed military means of defence, protection and ultimately counter-attack – and that means was *there*, just across the mountains, but was of no avail to them. And the guerrillas too, if they were not to die of hunger, or be shot down by the enemy (and hunger had desperately weakened every guerrilla's powers of physical resistance well before the army's bullets got to him), needed a social class to adopt them, feed and shelter them – yet that social class could do nothing for them. The guerrilla force sent a communiqué (the ELN's bulletin no. 5), calling on the miners to come to the mountains and join them, so as to carry on the fight in better conditions; but the message never reached the miners, for lack of means of communication. The absence of the most elementary political and material means meant that what was intended as an appeal became no more than an impossible wish. There was tragedy in this encounter-that-never-was, for each side was mutilated by the absence of the other: the guerrilla fighting was like a spearhead without any spear, a sharp point without a handle, with nothing that could be taken hold of by a socially ready collective user to make it the really effective missile it should have been. And the vanguard of the working class was like a wooden shaft without any steel at the end, a weapon with neither a point nor a cutting edge, quite without any military value even for self-defence. Could these two separate elements have been united there would have been a valuable class weapon, a genuine tool for victory. Could they have been united, or even coordinated.

The ruling class can always be counted on to be discerning whenever its interests and survival are at stake. And in this case what could have been a deadly enemy was in the process of coming into being. It seems as though the Barrientos–Ovando clique was more fully aware of the threat they would face if these two forces should combine than were the forces themselves. Certainly the protagonists of revolutionary action seemed either to underestimate or disregard the seriousness of their separation. Yet the convergence of their strategic interests, and the fact that the appearance of the guerrillas as an up-and-coming force (as they were in June) coincided so perfectly with the reappearance of the miners as a bastion of working-class resistance, were so amazingly obvious that the enemy could only take them for the result of a concerted plan, of previous political contacts. Alas, the enemy were wrong. Basically no such contacts had ever taken place. The miners and their families were machine-gunned in the completely erroneous belief that there was a 'subversive' conspiracy. But in fact, whenever the neo-colonial Bolivian bourgeoisie have wanted to call 'their' proletariat to order, and the risk did not seem great, they have never had any difficulty in finding a pretext.

The massacre of 24 June contained the seeds of the tragedy that was to come – the murder of 8 October. The same generals who had ordered the one ordered the other; and what made it possible for them to massacre the miners, without the guerrillas being able to prevent or deter them, was also what made it possible to murder Che, without the miners being able to prevent or deter them. The miners of Siglo Veinte and the guerrillas of the Vallegrande were made brothers in death by their inability to be brothers in life; they were fighting the same battle but they were not fighting it together, and so could not transform what was historically an alliance into a united action here and now. A study of this episode is therefore the first step in understanding the failure of the guerrillas.

It is foolish indeed to relegate the tragedy of 1967 to the archives of past history. It was an event which drew together all the threads of Bolivian history, thus in a sense symbolizing all of it; at the same time it represented a kind of miniature of the situation of all Latin America today.

It summed up the Bolivian class struggle which, as is clear from all recent events, is simply a repetition varying in tone and intensity of the funeral dirge of that terrible year – for there is still no convergence between the social reality of the people as a class and the political consciousness of the vanguard, between the activity of the unarmed masses 'below' and the interventions of the armed vanguard 'above', the spontaneous actions of the former, and the planned actions of the latter.

It summed up the fundamental problems of the Latin American class struggle in that what remains its most urgent need is to combine the art of defence with that of attack, tactics with strategy, economic and social demands with political and military needs. When the two pieces of this puzzle – basically complementary, but emerging in practice as alternative or mutually exclusive – the traditional dilemma of revolutionaries everywhere, can be fitted together, then we shall have a complete and recognizable picture of the Latin American revolution. The situation is more nearly ripe for achieving this in Bolivia than anywhere else. Che's guerrilla force, representing a huge historical step forward as it did, has brought considerably closer the point when a concrete, revolutionary solution will be found for these classic dilemmas.

I have used the images of the detonator and the explosive, of the small and large motors. But Che, though he used them, saw them as no more than what they are – convenient metaphors. They are no longer useful as instruments of analysis because they are trite (ten years' use will wear anything out), and fundamentally inaccurate (the social individuals who make up the class force are not an inert mass, nor is their dialectical interaction like the coupling of two motors). Some would also say that these metaphors are based on a definite assumption, accepting the postulates of the *foquista* theory, and cannot therefore be used in an objective analysis, since they take for granted the very thing that has to be proved: that the *foco*, given certain historical conditions, can act as a detonator, and dependent capitalism as a stick of TNT. In any case, like any image, these can only be used to *describe* something *static*. And the guerrilla war, even though its impetus was brought to a halt on 8 October, is above all a *dynamic* in which what happened in the past is taken up again in a plan for the future. It arises out of a definite past and endeavours to get beyond it to a definite future. To understand it, then, one must first look to the past and identify its concrete beginning, and then turn again to the future in that light, examining the various possibilities which determine its meaning and direction. Where did it come from? How did it take shape? What were its objectives? Only this factual history, with its inevitable attendant limitations, can bring that inert object back to life, and enable us to understand why, for instance, the action Che was forced to take seemed at times to contradict the theoretical notions Che himself had worked out in several of his writings. In a piece that is of special interest because it is written from the unusual point of view of a 'Bolivian revolutionary nationalist', René Zavaleta Mercado, we read: 'The Bolivian Che did not always stick to the rules of the theoretical Che, either generally or at specific moments, so that it could be said that Che actually denied the general theories of Che.'* This apparently incomprehensible hiatus between Che's general theory and his specific behaviour in Bolivia is just what it is most important to understand, for in a way it sums up in microcosm the whole richness of life, the movement of human history, everything daring and alive in human action. It is enormously significant.

There have been so many mystifying interpretations, such a mass of wordy perplexity and surprise, that the history of

* *La Frustración de Ñancahuazú*, October 1969.

the Bolivian Che has ended by being smothered in a pall of silence and confusion, thus turning into a kind of smouldering mystery a crucial experience which, whether they like it or not, is part of the historical inheritance of all Latin American militants, something they should all make their own. All too often people have looked at this whole story with a brief and jaundiced glance, forming a summary and rigid judgement of it; they sum up all the 'mistakes' and 'illusions' abstractly, without seeing them in perspective or understanding their internal logic, and then quite naturally dismiss them as 'unbelievable' and 'incomprehensible'. Here is one of many examples, taken from an otherwise intelligent and useful study:

It is hard to believe that so many mistakes could have been made by a group under the command of one of the greatest heroes of the Latin American revolution. Not merely errors of preparation (confusion between the training area and the zone of operations, carelessness in contacts, general haphazardness in the location of stores, in map-making, in supply systems, etc.), but also really fundamental errors: painful though it is, it must be admitted that Guevara made a major political mistake in trying to establish a political front in support of his *foco* out of bureaucrats and opportunists with the most disparate theoretical and strategic ideas, often belonging to divergent if not positively antagonistic groups.

And immediately after this, he continues:

Those mistakes were not foreseen by Debray, any more than was the extraordinary indifference shown by the Bolivian peasants to the heroism of the guerrillas.*

As to this, I should like to insert a brief parenthesis. I have often been given the honour of having my name linked with the groundwork for Che's Bolivian plan; and my *Revolution in the Revolution?* has been connected with the events of Ñancahuazú. The honour is quite undeserved. It goes without saying that Che did not ask my advice before deciding to set up his guerrilla *foco* in Bolivia. Nor did I

* 'Considérations sur les thèses de Régis Debray', Marcelo de Andrade, *Les Temps Modernes*, Paris, May 1969.

know which area he would ultimately choose to operate in, or rather establish the *foco* in, inside the country. I did not therefore foresee the indifference of the Bolivian peasants – first because there is no such entity as 'Bolivian peasants' in general, but only local groups differing from one region to another, and then because I was in no position to foresee, still less to decide, anything.

This being so, I think it no shame to admit that I did not foresee that Che's undertaking would fail; even though I was aware of certain weak links in the political structure of the guerrilla war at first, I felt confident that as the military actions developed, they would gradually be strengthened. Furthermore, I deny that that failure appeared fatal, or foreseeable, or even probable. John William Cooke once said that he would rather be wrong with Che Guevara than right with Vittorio Codovilla.* But he understated his case, for in the event both right and history were on Che's side. Unlike the Teoponte plan of 1970,† which looked doomed to failure before it began (that *was* foreseeable and I said so, though advice of that sort is seldom well received), the Ñancahuazú plan in 1967 seemed to follow a line that was possible, credible and worthy of confidence.

But we must give honour where it is due. The lamentable 'errors' of Che are reminiscent of the lamentable 'errors' of the Commune, and the lamentable astonishment of Marx's German correspondent, Kugelmann, shortly afterwards. Perhaps the best answer to this sort of retrospective prognostication is to quote Lenin's preface to the 1907 Russian edition of Marx's letters to Kugelmann (two years after the lamentable 'errors' of 1905):

He [Marx] grasps that any attempt to anticipate *precisely* in advance the fortunes of the struggle would be charlatanism or unpardonable self-confidence. *More than anyone* he recognizes the fact that the working class – heroically, self-denyingly and with a

---

* Cooke was a Peronist revolutionary leader who lived for a long time in Cuba. Codovilla was Secretary of the Argentine Communist Party. Both are now dead.

† See Political Chronology of Bolivia, p. 149.

spirit of initiative – *are the authors* of world history. Marx looked at history from the viewpoint of those who *make* it without having any way of knowing *infallibly* in advance their chances of success, not as a moralizing petty-bourgeois intellectual who can say, 'It was easy to foresee . . . Such and such should not have been done . . .'*

         * The italics are Lenin's.

2

From Rearguard to Vanguard

THE Bolivian Revolution of 1952 was an isolated but major event in Latin American history. Its later deterioration and the geographical isolation of the country gradually blurred its edges, until it was virtually forgotten in the collective consciousness of the continent, while the profoundly nationalist stamp of the uprising prevented its figuring on the worldwide revolutionary scene. However at the time it made all of Latin America shiver, either with fear or with hope.

In La Paz in 1953, a young, newly qualified Argentinian doctor with a taste for travel, Ernesto Guevara Lynch, was able to see for the first time a sight which the Peronist regime (to which the young Guevara, still faithful to his class and family background, was avowedly hostile) took care not to let the citizens of Argentina see: a people in arms who, led by the working class, had put down the revolt of an entire army in three days. When in Guatemala, a year later, Guevara enrolled in civil defence to fight against the invasion of Castillo Armas, and tried to arm action groups to defend Arbenz, his memories of Bolivia served him in good stead. But not until the Cuban Revolution was he to see a feat on the same scale: the physical destruction of a whole regime, starting with its spinal column, the armed forces, which was replaced by a popular militia. But this time the context was reversed. One could hold forth at length about such historical reversals, parallel but opposite in direction, about the strange twist of fate of a continuous revolutionary regression in which the proletariat lays the ground for an ideology and a political action of a petty-bourgeois kind, as in Bolivia, as compared with that continuous revolutionary progression in which the poor peasants and urban petty bourgeoisie lay the ground for a proletarian-oriented ideology and political action, as in Cuba. It is not without significance that Comandante Guevara, virtually a chance spectator of the former, and a protagonist in the latter, came back to die in the country where he had first sniffed the scent of revolution, that heady compound of gunpowder and human sweat.

Somehow, in a matter of ten years or so, the Bolivian proletariat was turned aside, pushed into the background and then violently removed from power; a popular revolution was turned inside out like a glove by the very men who had made it – first among them Paz Estenssoro – so as to become a counter-revolution. Somehow, the '9 April 1952' managed to incubate and feed and give birth to such a total dialectical negation as the *coup* of 4 November 1964, and set up such a pathetic puppet as Barrientos on the debris of a proletarian revolution. Yet it is important to remember that up to then, up indeed until 1965, Bolivia stood out among its neighbours as an extraordinary bastion of democracy, the only Andean nation in which the popular movement was not totally stifled. Despite the ever more paralysing grip of North America, despite the ever fiercer repression of the working class by the regime's political police (the *Control político* under San Román, and beyond him, the American embassy), despite the expulsion of the 'left wing' of the MNR – despite all this, Bolivia still, in the early sixties, presented the surprising picture of a nation where the workers' militias, though disorganized, were still armed, where a powerful trade-union movement had brought its leader Juan Lechín to the post of Vice-President of the republic, where several Marxist–Leninist parties could still, for what it was worth, act openly in full view of the law. Even inside the government and the party which dominated it, the MNR (Movimiento nacionalista revolucionario), there were many who retained a memory, a nostalgia even, for the popular and anti-imperialist beginnings of the regime, which resulted in a certain amount of collusion, a turning of blind eyes to underground activities taking place beyond the bounds of legality.

Bolivia has vast, in places unexplored, frontiers of desert land with five other countries. At that time, under a civilian government, there was a fairly flexible police system, and little in the way of material resources for checking on those entering and leaving the country; these temporary political advantages supplemented the permanent natural advantages of omnipresent routine administrative corruption, which could be said to have a publicly recognized scale of charges, as well as an old-established tradition of smuggling. It was thus hardly surprising that, around that time, a certain number of revolutionary groups from neighbouring countries found in Bolivia, if not a totally secure and inviolable sanctuary, at least the basic minimum conditions for establishing something like a behind-the-lines base. As Stalin wrote, in words several times repeated and developed by General Giap, 'to make real war you must be able to count on a solid rearguard'. A number of organizations wanting 'to make real war', or rather to establish 'real' guerrilla *focos* in Argentina, Peru and elsewhere, came spontaneously to see Bolivia as the best place to organize their rearguard. It was the only possible place: everywhere else on the continent the imperialist Holy Alliance was sharpening its knives, so there was no choice. Thus the Bolivian nationalist revolution, though now adopted by the reaction, was, unconsciously and in spite of itself, being made to play its part in the cause of proletarian internationalism.

In July 1963 one of Che's closest collaborators, indeed his right-hand man, Papi (Captain José María Martínez Tamayo), arrived in La Paz with a Colombian passport. He had already carried out one important mission in Guatemala during the October crisis. This time, Che had given him the job of establishing at Tarija, in southern Bolivia, an operations and supply base for his Argentinian friend Jorge Masetti, the former director of Prensa latina in Havana, and his guerrilla group, the future Ejército Guerillero del Pueblo (EGP). Masetti was Comandante 'Segundo', a nickname odd enough (borrowed from Don Segundo Sembra, a legendary Argentinian gaucho in the last century) to make it clear to those involved that Comandante 'Primero' was none other than Che himself. Though the preparations for the base, established north of Salta in Argentina, just south of the Bolivian border, went well, the guerrillas were caught by the Argentinian police before even starting to fight, and were disbanded and liquidated at the end of 1964. News of the failure of this plan, so dear to him, reached Che in Paris as he was passing through on his way to Africa in January 1965. Not only had Masetti himself died, but among those killed was the young captain of the rebel army, Hermes Peña, who was a kind of adopted son of Che's. 'Papi', who had asked in vain to be allowed to stay with the Argentinian guerrillas, then went back to Havana. He had been supported in his work in Bolivia by a number of then unknown young communists whose names were to become famous three years later. Also in November 1964, there arrived in La Paz an Argentinian archaeologist and folklore student, known in respectable society as Laura Gutiérrez: this was Tamara Bunke, or 'Tania'. In Havana, the previous March, Che had told her that Bolivia was her ultimate destination, and had made clear to her how important and lengthy her mission there was to be. A typical instance of Che's far-sightedness.

In 1963, shortly before guerrilla fighting began in Argentina, the Peruvian ELN (National Army of Liberation), which had barely entered political life, had suffered the defeat of Puerto Maldonado, where Javier Heraud was killed. This guerrilla force, a detachment of which had emerged not far from the Bolivian border in a small river port in the Peruvian jungle, also came from Bolivia, but unlike Masetti's Argentinian group, they were able to get back there after being discovered by the Peruvian army. But they could never have retreated through this totally unknown jungle and found their way back to the Beni department in Bolivia had it not been for the help and support of Bolivian collaborators, people who were then also unknown communists, and also destined later to be among Che's guerrillas at Ñancahuazú. In fact, the man who acted as guide to the survivors of Puerto Maldonado and literally saved their lives, was 'El Ñato', Julio Luis Méndez, the great all-rounder of the Bolivian guerrillas, and a survivor of the Yuro (he was finally killed on 15 November 1967). He was born in the town of Trinidad in the Beni, north of La Paz, and his knowledge of the area was unequalled.

The impetus of the Cuban revolutionaries who had settled there, and their coordination, in this way made it possible for these Argentinian and Peruvian guerrilla operations to get vital protection and support, mostly from among the rank and file of the Bolivian Communist Party. The Party leadership had facilitated matters by detailing numbers of well-trained and trustworthy young members for this sort of work. For them, it was a way of demonstrating that they were in no way hostile to the armed struggle, without actually having to get involved in it themselves in their own country. They gained the confidence of the Cuban Revolution by such means without having to change their own political line inside the Party; the revolutionary energy of the finest militants among the Young Communists was channelled outwards; at the same time this created a parallel security system which could, in case of need, respond to demands of various kinds. Undeniably such a policy involved the Party in certain risks. Internationally, above all: the Bolivian CP attracted the wrath of several neighbouring Parties, as for instance the Argentinian, which protested forcefully against 'foreign' interference at the time of the Masetti incident – a protest and a dispute which were partly responsible for the calling of a Conference of Latin American Communist Parties in Havana at the end of 1964. Indeed the Bolivian Party also approved the calling of the conference, since it could then reply to the accusations and remove the doubts of the Argentinian comrades. In fact, though, the risks to the Bolivian CP inside the country were far more serious, although they did not at the time realize it. For gradually coming into being within the Party was a kind of special branch, whose attention was directed outwards, and attracted more and more to forms of action quite beyond the Party line and its limits.

The leadership itself had begun by selecting the cadres it considered most competent and best trained ideologically (to resist 'adventurist' temptations, and the danger of being perverted by such dubious contacts), mainly from within the Young Communist League.

The YCL, set up in 1953, three years after the Party itself, is defined in its statutes as a 'group of young people with its own organic and independent structure, determined by the political line of the Party'. It was in no sense a movement or a splinter group, and had no intention of working 'against' the Party; it had no specific political platform, and despite certain urges to independence shown by its representatives at various international congresses in the Soviet Union, in Chile, at the International Union of Students session in Prague, and in Bulgaria – where they ostentatiously sat with the Cuban delegates and voted with them – it blindly followed the directives and trends of the Party leadership. Thus, for instance, the small vanguard group, who were to provide the foundations of the future Bolivian ELN when Che arrived, wisely kept out of the disputes raging at the end of 1964 which ended in the breaking away of a minority of the Central Committee, who took with them the majority of the working-class cells of the Party to form a new 'Marxist–Leninist' Party. This schism at first related to the national problems then under discussion rather than the international, rejecting the opportunism of the *camarilla*, as the dissidents nicknamed the leadership. Only with the arrival of Zamora, Bolivia's representative at the Prague session of the International Union of Students (who had been absent at the time of the initial rupture) did the new Party describe itself as pro-Chinese – a decision now so well established that the two Communist Parties in Bolivia are known as the *pekineses* and *moscovitas*.

However, this ideological silence did not mean either consent about fundamentals or total identification with the

Party. These young militants already differed from the Party leadership on a number of specific points arising out of the nature of their work and their human contacts: they had a more internationalist outlook, tended to favour direct offensive action, were trained in techniques of clandestine work, and were more familiar with the Cuban Revolution and its representatives.

I recall all this pre-history not just for its intrinsic interest, but because it is vital for understanding the nature of Che's political alliances in Bolivia. For it was during this period that the group that was to be with him at Ñancahuazú was taking shape; it was on the basis of the Peruvian and Argentinian experiences that Che was to recruit and choose his contacts; it was his belief in the work they had done that made him trust them. Inti Peredo, Coco Peredo, Rodolfo Saldaña, Jorge Vásquez Viana, Antonio Jiménez, El Ñato, Loyola Guzmán, and others – all those who provided the urban rearguard and the pioneers of the guerrilla vanguard – were among them: the founders of the Bolivian ELN. They came to the forefront naturally, for each one of them had a history which, by 1966, accredited him as a dedicated and trustworthy revolutionary. It is true that they all came from the ranks of the CP or the YCL; however, it was not as such that Che involved them in the preparations for Ñancahuazú, but as members of an underground support network which had already proved its worth. Ñancahuazú was the continuation of a well-established line of action, and Che was moving on to a further stage in a history whose foundations in Bolivia he had himself laid in the early sixties. It was no accident that the first Cuban comrade to arrive in Bolivia in March 1966, even before Pombo (Captain Harry Villegas) and Tuma (Lieutenant Carlos Coello, Che's 'personal aide' from Sierra Maestra days), was 'Papi'; nor was it by chance that he set to work with these particular men, to whom he was bound by long-standing friendship, and whose qualities he had himself had occasion to discover some years earlier. It was absolutely natural that the work of establishing the infrastructure of Che's guerrilla force should fall to these communist militants who were such old friends of the Revolution.

Experience has abundantly confirmed the wisdom of that choice. The best proof that Che was right to entrust himself to them was their own behaviour afterwards. But everything has its price, and Che, through them, was indirectly bound by the decisions made by the Party leadership (and eventually bound hand and foot by them), for he had to make negotiations with them his first priority. Why? Because that was the moral and political support he had to offer in return for the collaboration of those who committed themselves alongside him to positions that were in flat contradiction to those of their Party. All were militants disciplined by, and hitherto blindly faithful to, their leadership. Gradually, as the revolutionary commitment of these comrades grew deeper, as they became not just collaborators but active guerrilla fighters, so the sensitive problem of their relationship with their Party became more acute. Che and his friends had good reason to believe that if the commitment to the principles and strategy of the armed struggle being demanded of them became incompatible with their loyalty to the Party, its discipline and its leadership, the consequence would be friction, agonizing heart-searching and doubts which could seriously compromise work already begun. If he was to make certain of this central core of Bolivians, he must win the Party over to the armed struggle; these comrades would then no longer feel themselves out on a limb. Thus, it was basically because of his moral obligation to Inti and the rest to 'cover' them with the leadership to which they were in theory subordinate, and to make clear once and for all their position as militants, that Che decided to take the step of making his first political contacts with Monje, the Secretary General, and the other members of the Political Commission, even though he did not particularly respect or trust them – especially since the Masetti disaster in 1964.

Moisés Guevara's group* did not present the same prob-

*See Chronology of Che in Bolivia, p. 153.

lems since, even before the first contacts had been made with them, they had already been expelled from the Marxist–Leninist CP, and formally condemned by Oscar Zamora's leadership. These dissidents from the 'Chinese' Party did not therefore have to give any account of their decisions to anyone else, and were in an autonomous position, unlike Inti and his comrades from the 'Soviet' Party.

Hence, Che's decision to make the CP his chief partner in the preparatory stages did not represent any particular stance, or personal option, or political affinity on his part (nor on anyone else's, for Fidel and the rest of the Cuban revolutionary leadership never made a move without Che's explicit approval, or one that did not respond to his wishes or decisions). It is clear that Che intended to make contact gradually, later on, with all existing organizations – 'including that of Lechín Oquendo'.* And 'including that of Zamora', we may add, for Papi was on very friendly terms with Zamora personally, outside Monje's party, though he never confided in him as to any political plan. The two had met in Havana in 1964, where Zamora was one of a delegation of Bolivian students. According to Zamora, Che had come to agree with him that the 1964 affair had been prematurely exposed through the fault of the Bolivian Party, and gave full moral support to an ideological and political struggle within the Party to attempt to change the leadership, draw together all vanguard elements and establish an infrastructure for the armed struggle. These aims were gradually dissipated as Zamora moved away from the path he had traced out when with Che; when he took over as head of a new party, he became totally absorbed in an international battle between party machines, under the auspices of China. Events thus took a different turn from what Che had envisaged.

None the less, it can still be said that at the *personal* level

* 'Pombo's Diary', 24 October 1966. This diary is printed in Daniel James (ed.), *The Complete Bolivian Diaries of Che Guevara, and Other Captured Documents* (Stein & Day, New York, 1968).

Che would undoubtedly have preferred at first to work with Zamora rather than Monje. But it must also be admitted that his active collaboration with the dissident group of Moisés Guevara, which had been expelled as a splinter group from Zamora's Marxist–Leninist Party, obviously did not help relations between Che and Zamora. At the end of 1966, in La Paz, Papi had a very clear impression (as he later told me) that Zamora was systematically avoiding him by failing to turn up at several meeting-places. Zamora himself maintains that his help had never been officially asked for by Papi, and that since he had never been informed as to the real purpose of his presence in Bolivia, he believed that, as in 1964, the Cubans in La Paz were there simply to sustain the revolutionary action taking place in Argentina. He therefore felt no obligations towards Papi other than those of ordinary friendship. Zamora was later captured and deported, but his party preserved the same attitude of suspicion and watchfulness towards the urban guerrilla group as the Communist Party under Monje. In either case, the choice of Monje as the main contact in the early stages did not by any means represent a refusal to communicate with other political groups or forces, but merely the inevitable result of a series of personal commitments and a collaboration of several years' standing at grass-roots level.

That this situation was dangerous there can be no doubt. First, it was impossible to evaluate the Party's leadership through the distorting glass of one small support group which, though originally selected by them, had taken shape on its own. It was impossible to judge the whole by one part, the Party itself as a whole by one group of militants, without taking into account political and ideological variables determined by the national and international conditions then prevailing in the workers' movement. Second, all the attention being paid to the Party, all the efforts being made to make favourable changes in its political line, were so much attention and effort *not* being given to other Parties, other groups representing the popular movement, with all of which it should have been vital to have the closest relations well worked out at various levels in advance (PRIN, sections of the MNR, the Marxist–Leninist CP, POR, and so on).*

The relations so painfully maintained with the leaders of the Bolivian CP were disastrous not only because of their results, or rather lack of results, but also, and possibly indeed more so (in my view at least), because it was impossible to combine them with what could have been valuable initiatives in other directions. Since every minute counted, since Che had decided to start fighting then and there without further ado, despite the still rudimentary nature of his Bolivian rearguard, his talks with the CP can be seen in retrospect as an irreparable waste of time, for their purpose

* This would undoubtedly have meant finding a friendly solution to an old dispute which would otherwise compromise this necessary relationship. In January 1966, a Bolivian delegation from the PRIN, Lora's POR and the Marxist–Leninist Party, represented respectively by Lydia Gueller, Lora. and Ruiz González, arrived uninvited in Havana, but were not allowed to take part in the Tricontinental Conference, and had to go home. This unfortunate (and in my opinion, regrettable) decision was apparently part of the price that had to be paid for the by-then established collaboration with the militant comrades of the CP under Monje's leadership. Like it or not, such organizations were quite as representative of actually existing popular forces as the Communist Party of Bolivia, if not more so. If a guerrilla force was to be established and develop among the people, then *all* popular organizations must be reckoned with, especially those most present within the working class – as those three parties were. At that stage, however, Bolivia was still no more than a rearguard, more technical than political in nature, for the guerrilla warfare Che envisaged as taking place outside the country – which explains why he then made that decision whose consequences were so immeasurable.

This incident was later to provide some with an argument and others with an excuse for believing that they had been rejected or undervalued by Che's group. The proof that those organizations, especially their militant sectors, constituted a reserve of available forces is that, despite their differences, when the time came Lechín's PRIN, and to a lesser extent Lora's POR demonstrated their sympathy and solidarity with the guerrillas in words and at times action; and there were many among the grass roots of Zamora's party who tried hard to make contact with ELN members in La Paz to offer them help, and even to join in the actual fighting.

was the unattainable one of gaining the Party's support for the war. Evidently it was right to deal with the Party leadership – it would have been impossible not to do so. What was deplorable was that by the time that had been done, the possibility of establishing relations with the other available political forces had been to all intents and purposes lost. The CP thus found itself in the position of arbiter, and, aware of the key role they played because of being the first and therefore privileged partners in discussion, the Party leaders made the talks drag on so as to keep the monopoly of contacts in their hands for as long as possible. Monje's overriding determination was not to complete the military preparations, or even to establish his political positions, but to ensure that the other political forces, particularly the rival Marxist–Leninist Party, did not know what was happening. He even went so far as to insist that his own participation must depend on the exclusion both of Zamora's Communist Party and Moisés Guevara's splinter group. With incredible narrow-mindedness and chauvinism, the Bolivian CP made the utmost use of its relationship with the Cuban Revolution for objectives that were narrowly partisan and not revolutionary at all: it was more important to put down rival or allied organizations than to reinforce the revolutionary work that was going on. This petty in-fighting, which turned what could have been positive help from the Cuban Revolution into a kind of political trophy to be used by one party in crushing its neighbours, is sadly typical of what happens all too often in Latin America.

It seems as though, until mid-1966, Che saw Bolivia simply as a point of departure for Peru, where he actually hoped to go in order to join the guerrilla forces already established there. Papi had been given instructions at the beginning of his mission which leave us in no doubt that such was the original plan; that is why the underground infrastructure in La Paz was from the first based on members of the Peruvian ELN who had settled in the country after the Puerto Maldonado affair. But the defeat suffered

by Luis de la Puente at Mesa Pelada in Cuzco, together
with the loss of the group of Lobatón and Máximo Velando
in Junín, sealed for the short term the fate of the MIR as a
military organization; and the Tincoj ambush in December
1965, followed by the capture of Héctor Béjar, did the same
for the ELN. These setbacks in 1965, which were confirmed
in the early months of 1966, really did away with Che's
first option. The Peruvian ELN had slowly to re-build itself
– to which task Juan Pablo Chang, 'El Chino', set himself
with methodical fervour, and with the help of the cadres
of his organization then in Bolivia.

In any case, the fight in Peru could only begin again from
a base in Bolivia; this was Che's own conclusion, and it was
this that Papi and Pombo had to get Sánchez to convey to
the Peruvians in La Paz in June. Even though it only meant
a delay in the plans for Peru, this bad news inevitably
caused a certain disappointment and resentment among the
Peruvians – though they overcame them fairly quickly.
Bolivia, on the other hand, having up to then been a rearguard for the various sections of the guerrilla army developing on a continental scale, suddenly became the actual area
of operations, the objective of Che's guerrilla plans, and
the hub of his political and military activities. To the
astonishment of the Bolivian Communist Party, discon-
certed by this unforeseen turn of events, the Bolivian network which had up to then been working in the rearguard
as a support system moved directly into the foreground as
the base of operations. The die was cast.

3

Class and Power Relations in Bolivia

I MUST here insert a parenthesis to account for a certain oddity – the apparent symptom of a possible contradiction; though a personal digression, this should make it possible to delve a bit more deeply into objective history. I have for some years been ritually accused of *foquismo*, castigated, and dragged in sackcloth and ashes through innumerable pages of print. With both friends and enemies assuming that I carry this particular flag, both tend to hold me to some extent ideologically responsible for the *foco* of Ñancahuazú. On many counts, as I have said, it is an honour I do not deserve. But political myths of this kind are indestructible: existing in the sphere of the imaginary, beyond truth and falsehood, they are of their nature incapable of proof or disproof. Some observers however have had the honesty to point out that in one small published work I did recently exclude Bolivia from the area of effectiveness of rural guerrilla forces in Latin America; but they could not in that case understand what I could have been doing in a rural guerrilla *foco* in Bolivia! Was it inconsistency or out-and-out contradiction?

Anyone who witnessed the agony of the democratic revolution in the early sixties, as I did, must have recognized that that country, as far as it was possible to judge, constituted the weakest link in the chain of imperialist domination in Latin America. 'Bolivia is the country where the subjective and objective conditions are best combined. It is the only country in South America where a socialist revolution is on the agenda, despite the reconstitution of an army which was totally destroyed in 1952.' I wrote that at the end of 1964, in a critical analysis of the *foquista* experiment in Latin America* in which Che took some interest at

* 'Castroism: the Long March in Latin America', in *Strategy for Revolution*, Cape, 1970, p. 38.

the time (and before the said army had appeared to take over the popular rising of 4 November and turn it into a military counter-revolution). In that piece I took as my premise, with all the needful reservations and clarifications, the rule given by Che himself in his book, *Guerrilla Warfare*, that 'in underdeveloped America, the countryside is the basic area for armed fighting'; but I could not fail to point out the uniqueness of the 'Bolivian case', which seemed to me to give the lie to Che's axiom since there, though it would have been tactically possible, it would have been strategically dangerous. For it was the very things which made Bolivia the 'weakest link' that also made it necessary to abandon the *foquista* concept as the main axis of the struggle. And I added, immediately after the sentence I have just quoted,

It is also the only country where the revolution might take the classic Bolshevik form – witness the proletarian insurrection of 1952 on the basis of 'soviets', which 'exploded' the state apparatus by means of a short and decisive armed struggle. The theory of the *foco* is thus in Bolivia, for reasons of historical formation which are unique in America, if not inadequate, at any rate secondary.

How could a man put forward such a view and find himself later condemned to thirty years' detention in that same country as a 'murderer, thief and bandit' (to quote the flattering terms of the judge's sentence), or more soberly, as someone who had been to some extent involved with the rural *foco* of Ñancahuazú?

I would like to explain the reasons for thinking that Bolivia was in fact not amenable to any *foquista* system, and also the reasons why such an observation did not basically invalidate Che's plans for guerrilla warfare. To do this, I must begin with at least a superficial examination of the social and historical situation in Bolivia.

Bolivian classicism

Whatever the mishaps which may have actually brought it about, the choice of Bolivia, 'Bolívar's favourite daughter', as the base for a new Bolívar-style project, was not inopportune or even arbitrary, but profoundly reasonable. In addition to the obvious geographical advantages of a country in the centre of South America, with access to five other countries, and a commanding position in relation to the whole 'southern cone' of the continent, there were even more forceful reasons of a historical nature. What Engels wrote at the end of the last century about France* in relation to the rest of Europe could be said today of Bolivia in relation to the rest of Latin America. Bolivia 'is the land where, more than anywhere else, the historical class struggles were each time fought out to a decision, where, consequently, the changing political forms within which they occur and in which their results have been summarized have likewise been stamped with the sharpest outlines'. And indeed, where, on this continent, can we find more clear-cut forms of political domination than in this country – with its ability to pass in a matter of days from one extreme to the other, from the beginnings of a dictatorship of the proletariat to a fully developed military fascism?

But the 'classical purity' Engels saw in the French struggle, and especially in the domination of the French bourgeoisie, only applies here to the historical role of the exploited; it is not true of the exploiters. True, in Bolivia, 'the struggle of the upward striving proletariat against the ruling bourgeoisie has also appeared here in an acute form unknown elsewhere', but the bourgeoisie does not rule in Bolivia in the classic form. On the contrary: it is the social backwardness and political impoverishment of the bourgeoisie in a dependent and undeveloped capitalist country which appears in its classic form there. The struggle of the proletariat takes on the most extreme forms precisely because the inability of the bourgeoisie to fulfil its historical role as a 'national class' is more total there than anywhere else. In other words, Bolivia is the classical example *not* of a country in which an old bourgeoisie has set its seal on all

* Preface to the third German Edition of Marx's *Eighteenth Brumaire of Louis Bonaparte*, 1883.

social development, but of an agrarian country which, though backward, is dominated by the capitalist world market, and where it falls to a young and forceful proletariat to fulfil the historical tasks left undone by the bourgeoisie. In this sense, it is the whole of present-day Bolivian society which is really a historical metaphor – a bit of the past carried over into the present, a bit of Europe carried over to America, its own special characteristics standing out sharply and presented to the observer under laboratory conditions. It is a Russia of 1905 in miniature, transplanted to Indo-America in the era of the decline of imperialism: that is what Bolivia would look like from outside to the detached gaze of the entomologist of history judging from its morphology, so to say, before starting on any internal analysis, any study of the anatomy of the subject under observation. That is why all the concepts, the arguments and even the slogans of the original, i.e. European, Marxist tradition have fallen on such good ground in Bolivia; they are not like things transplanted from outside at all, but things that have actually grown up there – things, if you like, that Bolivia has re-created for itself. For decades now, Mensheviks, Bolsheviks, revolutionary socialists and anarcho-syndicalists have been arguing away at the foot of the Illimaní and on the shores of Lake Titicaca. And their talk has not been the armchair intellectualizing of postgraduate students: these arguments have extended to local trade-union centres, the pitheads of the mines, the floor of the *Congresos populares*.

The foundations of 'permanent revolution'

The democratic, working-class movement of the country would not be so completely at home with that terminology, with those options, if this originally Marxist vocabulary were not profoundly expressive of the life of the country and the material living conditions of its people. One only really assimilates what is adapted to one's own needs. How, for instance, explain the continuing Trotskyist tendency among rank-and-file workers which has set its seal on the thinking of the trade-union movement from its beginnings, if the Bolivian revolution does not, in many of its objective aspects, illustrate the theories of permanent revolution outlined by Trotsky after 1905? Indeed, the most obvious characteristic of the Bolivian economic and social structure is the law of *uneven and combined development* on which those theories were based. Like a great many underdeveloped countries on to which the most advanced capitalist structures have been grafted, like Russia before the revolution, Bolivia presents an example of the most primitive production relationships existing alongside the most developed ones. Together with areas of agricultural subsistence economy, which were, up until 1953, dominated by pre-capitalist production relationships, there has been developing since the twenties a modern mining sector, intensely concentrated (in three groups, Patino, Hochschild and Aramayo, which were later nationalized), and directly integrated into the world market. Bolivia thus came late but wholeheartedly to capitalism, moving at a single leap to the most developed stage of capital without having gone through any of the intermediate stages. This historical contrast, resulting from the telescoping and overlapping of various forms of production which would normally have been successive and distinct, began to be less sharp in 1952; the 'National Revolution' tried, mainly by means of agrarian reform, to integrate its backward agricultural sector into a total national market economy; even so, the change was not fundamental. The nationalization of the tin mines, which replaced private monopolies with State capitalism, merely accentuated class antagonism, and made it inevitable that the economic demands of the mining proletariat should appear to be a political struggle to gain control of the State (for though there was still an active private sector, it remained on the sidelines, and the majority of all mining depended on the nationalized firm 'Comibol').

Here, more than anywhere, it would be blind indeed to substitute demography and anthropology for a historical study of the whole complexity of this particular social formation. European anthropologists classify the Bolivian population racially: 30 per cent Aymara natives, 32 per cent Quechua natives, and about 30 per cent mestizos or *cholos*. In fact, the racial identity of an individual largely depends on his economic and cultural status, and there are a multitude of steps in the social hierarchy of a population in which Indian and Spanish features merge into a single whole. The problem of whether Bolivia is a 'multi-national state' (in the fashionable phrase used in the outline programme which the Third Congress of the Bolivian CP adopted in June 1971) made up of ten or so oppressed native tribes, or whether, on the contrary, there already exists, even though as yet only imperfectly coordinated, a national state of Bolivia (in terms of the classic thesis of the theorists of *movimientista* nationalism), is part of an old and interminable controversy; it is, literally, interminable, because we simply have not got the conceptual tools to deal with what is known in Marxist tradition as the 'national problem' in any definitive way. In either case, the historical paradox of Bolivia consists in the juxtaposition of a 'native' farming population (in which, of course, there are differences as between language, area, and social position) predominant in numbers, but economically secondary and politically subordinate, and a far smaller proletariat whose economic function is central, and whose political role predominates.

Because of its position in the social process of production, the importance of the proletariat in the class structure is out of all proportion to its size. This universal law can be applied to all countries, but in Bolivia it is perhaps uniquely obvious. In 1965, the mineworkers represented 2·7 per cent of the working population, as compared with 48·7 per cent employed in agriculture and stock-breeding. Yet in 1966, the miners accounted for 94 per cent of all export earnings; in 1967, 77 per cent; and in 1968, 83 per cent. In 1967, of a total of $144m., tin alone accounted for $90m., and the other mining products (wolfram, silver, copper, antimony, lead and zinc) for $37m. In other words, it was basically the 30,000 tin miners who supported a country of five million inhabitants. This uneven and combined development of the productive forces of the country was expressed in a disproportionate development of some social forces to the detriment of others, of the proletariat to the detriment of the peasants and the national bourgeoisie.

This latter class is both less bourgeois and less national than in any other country in the hemisphere. Less bourgeois, because it has only recently emerged from the shadow of the landed proprietors (as was made clear as long ago as 1946 in the 'Tesis de Pulacayo', the first document produced by the unified workers' movement, adopted by the Federation of Mining Workers of Bolivia at their first Congress, which coined the term 'feudal bourgeoisie' to describe the then ruling class), and now lives by milking the administration and government, in the shadow of that concentrate of State bureaucracy – the armed forces. And less national, because more than any bourgeoisie elsewhere it depends for its economic livelihood, its political survival and its military superiority on the protection and aid of North American imperialism. This extreme weakness of the Bolivian bourgeoisie as a ruling class has always made it unable to effect a successful democratic-bourgeois revolution, and identify with the over-riding interests of the nation as against foreign control. Consequently, the role of 'national class' has fallen by default to the proletariat. The traditional tasks of the bourgeoisie – national independence, the abolition of huge landed estates, the unification of the domestic market, centralization of State administration, effective separation of Church and State, genuine universal education, etc. – cannot be achieved in a narrow framework of bourgeois domination. This is proved by the fact that those tasks could only be begun, if not completed, under firm pressure from the proletariat – and in part, under their control – after the 1952 revolution. The nationalizing of the mines, for instance, did not figure either in the MNR programme or in the intentions of Paz Estenssoro, who in fact publicly rejected the idea before his return from exile after the rising. This essential reform was only achieved, on the terms of 'nationalization without compensation and under workers' control', under pressure from the people, and especially the proletariat – whose wishes were made known inside the government by Juan Lechín, Executive Secretary of the COB (Bolivian Workers' Confederation).

For all these tasks to be successfully undertaken the proletariat, without abandoning its alliance with the petty bourgeoisie, would have had to take over the leadership of that class alliance. What in fact happened was precisely the reverse: bit by bit the *Cogobierno obrero* of 1952 degenerated into the out-and-out subordination of the COB to the bureaucracy controlled by the petty bourgeoisie of the MNR. Indeed, the achievement of the aims of democracy in itself results in putting the aims of socialism, so to speak, on the agenda. One can thus see how a combined development of the aims of bourgeois democracy and those of socialism at the level of economic productive forces is ultimately what determines their combined development at the level of politically productive social forces. One also sees how the theory of permanent revolution gained authority and credibility with a large section of the workers' movement; by this theory, put forward by Trotsky after 1905 and developed up to 1929 in his book, *The Permanent Revolution*, the dictatorship of the proletariat is defined as the means towards national democracy rather than its goal.

One of his theses in particular, being extremely broad in scope, seems to fit the present-day Bolivian revolution to a T, and few responsible workers would reject it: 'For countries with an undeveloped bourgeoisie, especially colonial and semi-colonial countries, the theory of permanent revolution means that the proper and complete fulfilment of their aims for democracy and national liberation can only be the dictatorship of the proletariat, taking over the leadership of the oppressed nation, and above all of the peasant masses.' And, finally, one sees how in such a perspective the Leninist slogan, 'Democratic dictatorship of the workers and peasants', can be interpreted and distorted, so that the permanent revolution becomes 'a dictatorship of the proletariat drawing the mass of the peasants *behind* it'. Though this looks like no more than a verbal distinction, in fact everything hinges on it – and tacking the democratic petty bourgeoisie of the towns on at the end does not really make any difference.

As we know, the fate of the workers' movement and the socialist revolution in Russia between 1903 and 1917 (and beyond) hung *for all practical purposes* on theoretical subtleties of interpretation of this kind, which represented what was basically at stake in the various in-fighting between Mensheviks and Bolsheviks. Is this also true of the Bolivian revolution? The Bolivia of 1950 could perhaps be described, like Russia in 1905, as 'pregnant with two revolutions, but incapable of giving birth to the first, the national bourgeois one, without producing the second, the socialist one'. If so, it seems reasonable to carry the comparison to its logical conclusion and say that, as in Russia after 1905, the problem of transforming the original national bourgeois revolution into a socialist proletarian revolution depended on the treatment of the problem of the respective positions of the poor peasants and the impoverished urban petty bourgeoisie in relation to the dominant proletariat.

All that has happened in recent Bolivian history goes to indicate that, despite their superior numbers, the peasants have never managed to play any independent, or even active, part in politics alongside the other classes. Yet this does not mean that the countryside is in a state of peace. Nothing could be less placid than the Cochabamba valley, for example. If statistics were available, they would include several dozens of dead – some shot – in all country districts every month. The legendary vendetta between the neighbouring communities of Cliza and Ocureña, the armed conflicts among rival caciques, communities, or trade-union factions, the sporadic 'explosions' of the peasant militia, or what is left of them, the sudden outbursts of 'Indian anger' against the abuses and generally arbitrary behaviour of the local administrative authorities – all these certainly represent class antagonisms and a latent state of social ferment.

The existence now in the La Paz area of the 'Túpaj Katarí' – a movement that is indigenist and almost separatist, and demanding participation in public affairs for the Aymara and Quechua people in terms of their own cultural roots and through their own representatives – is quite enough to show that the magnificent tradition of rebellion, against the colonial power in the past and against republican aristocracy in the last century, is not totally dead.* But today, such acts of violent protest, though symptomatic of an endemic and widespread unrest, are not characterized by revolutionary, or even pre-revolutionary, agitation, except perhaps in a few places where progressive political cadres from the towns have been able to exert their influence. These scattered elements of social struggle cannot be combined into the beginnings of a civil war. Despite their episodic ferocity, they remain what I can only call infra-political.

In Vietnam, the capacity for national and popular resistance against foreign invasion and oppression is based on that infinitely complex mosaic or filigree of autonomous village communities which extends over the entire territory, from the Delta to the mountains in the interior. That 'mosaic' has from time immemorial constituted the infrastructure of the country's economic, social, religious and political life – and therefore, if need be, its military infrastructure too. In Bolivia, on the other hand, the centre of gravity of the nation's life is not in the country areas. The traditional Indian communities have been broken up, dispossessed, and taken over by the power first of Spain, then

---

* The former is best symbolized by the names of Túpac Amaru, Indian chief of Pampamarca in Peru, who led a rebellion from November 1870 to May 1872 against the Spanish colonists, and Túpaj Katarí, leader of a nineteenth-century Indian rebellion in which La Paz was besieged; the latter by the name of General Manuel Isidoro Belzu, President of Bolivia in 1848 and the first representative of popular nationalism in the post-colonial era.

of the Republic, so that they could no longer develop as total entities; this became even more the case after the 1952 agrarian reform and the increasing fragmentation of such land as was cultivable, in combination with the weight of age-old apathy.

In addition to these economic and social factors resulting from years of wastage of the original resources of the country, there is a specific ecological factor which also militates against a guerrilla war: the peasants rooted in their ancestral soil are concentrated on the high rocky plateaux, or the enclosed valleys round Cochabamba where the climate is temperate, leaving the areas of tropical forest near the borders of the country virtually deserted. Thus history and nature in Bolivia have worked together to produce a peculiarly difficult form of social geography in which, as René Zavaleta says, 'where there are trees there are no people, and where there are people there are no trees'. Che's guerrilla forces, including the young apprentice-guerrillas of Teoponte, were to suffer the inevitable and disastrous consequences of this unhappy situation.

We can see, then, that the industrial proletariat (and small artisans) came to the forefront of the political and social scene on the Altiplano as much through the weakness of the peasants as an organic class force as by their own strength. Obviously the Bolivian proletariat are not alone: their function as theoretical vanguard of the socialist revolution is shared with their fellows all over underdeveloped Latin America, including those places where the poor and middle peasants are forceful enough to help keep in being and support the upkeep of an urban and petty-bourgeois guerrilla group. But unlike those countries (Colombia, Guatemala, Venezuela, and perhaps Peru), the Bolivian proletariat combine their theoretical leadership role with a practical role as protagonists in revolutionary action: they are there in the front line *themselves* – not by delegation or proxy or through any third party. Indeed they make so bold as to manage without the usual intermediaries, the authorized spokesmen of the working class who, according to Kautsky and Lenin's theory of organization, represent their long-term historical interests. They are so pigheaded as to refuse to delegate their powers or their representation to the petty-bourgeois intelligentsia who, everywhere else, are ready to present the working class with their revolutionary party, its political workers, and the Marxist knowledge they carry with them wherever they go.

In Bolivia the proletariat carry their own ideological luggage themselves, and fulfil their own historical mission; they do it in their day-to-day lives, in the direct, harsh, and certainly not very refined form of the trade-union meeting which in this sense may be defined as a specific mode of political self-management. And they have recourse to industrial action not just as a reformist class, in order to negotiate with their exploiters the conditions under which they are prepared to sell their labour, but also, when occasion arises, as a revolutionary class, working to create the political conditions in which there will no longer be any buying or selling of labour. In other words, the proletariat, as a class whose specific social condition epitomizes the condition of all exploited people, is a *leading force*. As a class allied with the impoverished and politically aware petty bourgeoisie (artisans, low-paid white-collar workers, underemployed wage-earners, NCOs in the armed services, school-teachers, university and high-school students, the unemployed in the shanty-towns), it is a *moving force*. But as a class deluded as to its own political importance and with an overweening self-confidence, caught up in a political situation in which the national petty bourgeoisie has taken the poor peasants away from it as a social and political ally, the proletariat has been drawn into playing a role it cannot sustain, trying to fill a void that is too large for it; it has tried to become the *principal force*, on its own. It is then that it is doomed to failure. It is then that it provides the revolution not only with all its ideas, but also with all its dead; and it is the bodies of those isolated and despairing martyrs which have strewn Bolivia's road to socialism since 1960.

The dangers of 'permanent revolution'

The date 1960 more or less marks the point at which the working class withdrew into itself to protest against the policy of national and social treason pursued by the ruling MNR (the breakaway of the 'left wing' of the party in power, and establishment of the PRIN under the leadership of Juan Lechín). What then became quite clear – from the setbacks, massacres, lockouts, and wage-reductions forced upon the workers after that – was the inability of the working class to wage a successful fight for power, or even for the defence of their own immediate interests, in isolation from other oppressed and exploited classes: the poor peasants and agricultural proletariat whether altiplano or cruzeño, *kolla* or *camba*, and the urban petty bourgeoisie.

This *de facto* isolation of the proletariat was certainly not chosen by them, and they were the first to suffer from it. However, somehow or other it became the object of an ideological 'processing' which turned it into a *de jure* isolation, so to say, which the victims themselves fostered and kept in being. What happened was that the objectively dominant role allotted to the mining and industrial proletariat was reflected, at the level of the spontaneous awareness of the sophisticated proletariat, in a fierce ouvrierism; it was the one-sided and illusory reflection of a class supremacy which, though there was some basis for it, only expressed a partial truth, a one-sided truth; it was, in other words, a mistaken vision. That systematized and, in its own terms, coherent, ouvrierism does not reflect the inner totality and profound unity of the social reality of Bolivia, but only the surface split between a minority vanguard class and a majority rearguard class which at first sight look like separate segments of a disparate social whole. Ouvrierism seems to be a decoy, a trap in which uneven and combined development catches the workers' movement and deadens its awareness of itself and its relationship to other classes. It is the ideology which corresponds to the relatively isolated social situation of a concentrated industrial proletariat from a peasant class far larger in numbers but scattered, compartmentalized, heterogeneous, lacking in organic unity and consequently marginal. As such, it fulfils to perfection all that is demanded of an ideological function, by at once rationalizing, hiding and sublimating the social identity of the class in its own eyes. By a piece of ideological mystification, the proletariat's position of superiority develops into a kind of superiority complex; the class becomes cut off in 'splendid isolation', ready to be imperious if not positively imperial towards its allies, who are never allowed to forget the ignominy of their petty-bourgeois origins when they need calling to order.

The implacable logic of ouvrierism, by equating class origin with class position, ends by rebounding against its own proponents, enclosing the working class within itself, paralysing its capacity for political action, making it beyond its power to confront genuine class differences as they really are and to pay the price of a political alliance. Hence an inferior 'marginal' class, like the peasants, finds the proletariat no longer offering dialogue and guidance, but merely providing support from the opposite end of the social horizon as a superior 'marginal' class, if one may use such a phrase. Dialogue between the two is no longer possible, and the political utterances of the working class, which could be the universalizing and totalizing focus of national demands, become a monologue in the desert where a single and solitary class listens smugly to the echo of its own voice. Thus we find an inverse aristocracy of the working class coming into being – and I use the term in its revolutionary rather than its reformist sense – the specific product of imperialist exploitation, but produced by the exploited, and not the exploiters.

There is nothing astonishing about this paradox. The reversal of perspectives and proportions will seem to the supporters of permanent revolution as one more consequence, odd but logical, of uneven and combined development. Where a country is backward, the proletariat will be advanced; where a country is advanced, the proletariat will be backward (too perfect a formula to be valid, but not without relevance in the context of the North American metropolis and its relationship with its Bolivian satellite). This anomaly did not escape Che Guevara, and if my memory serves me right, to the extent that he anticipated the negative repercussions it might have in a period of transition to socialism, he felt considerable fear for the future.

Without going quite so far into the realms of hypothesis, but sticking to known fact, we can understand how such a dialectical paradox, the product of a complex historical development, could, though captivating to the imagination, be misleading in a confrontation with reality: here we have a nation which by all recognized statistics is at the bottom of the ladder of development alongside Haiti and Paraguay (in 1968, the average income was $158 a year, 65 per cent of the population were illiterate, and so on); yet its workers' movement is the most politically advanced on the continent, and qualitatively, in terms of its maturity and the scope of its ideological subtleties and inner variations, can bear comparison with those of France and Italy. Indeed, though that workers' movement has grown up out of the national reality itself, it has none the less in a sense turned its back on that national reality, at least as economically and demographically defined.

This disregard of its own origins and of society as a whole in the workers' movement is expressed in two ways – two major ideological and organizational derivations: anarcho-syndicalism, the dominant and numerically stronger tradition, and a Trotskyist trend which owes its persistent influence, despite endless fragmentation, to its talent for theorizing and for journalistic publicity. The two are irreconcilable, since the former worships at the shrine of workers' spontaneity, while the latter is based on political organization sustained by a clear programme. But, despite themselves, they converge at one point: both, whether consciously or otherwise, leave out of account what Leninist tradition calls 'the national and peasant problem'. I need not analyse the causes of this phenomenon, but would merely note that in an oppressed and dependent nation, where there is the further complication of an extremely heterogeneous population, whose way of life is predominantly agricultural, to dignify that omission by making it a political line is, to say the least, not the wisest policy. We have seen that this relegation, this underestimation, is not due to the whim or the dogmatism of some dedicated ideologist: there is an undeniable basis for it in fact, and it is that which makes it ineradicable. Though I am by-passing 1967 to look at the guerrilla war and its significance in the light of later events, it is not just a coincidence that the proletarian paradigms of the Petrograd Soviet and the 'dual power' of 1917 should have made the town of La Paz the scene for their first appearance, their first reincarnation, so to speak, in Latin America; the forms they have taken – the MNR – *Cogobierno obrero* of 1952 and the Popular Assembly of 1971 – are somewhat different, but present very much the same precariousness and confusion. Those paradigms did not fall out of a clear sky; they rose from the depths – specific depths, perhaps, considered from a particular aspect – of Bolivian political history and social organization. But nor was it a coincidence that, unlike the Russian model of the past, the Bolivian carbon copy should have survived for so short a time. The two occasions when an attempt was made to achieve 'dual power' failed because they did not include the poor peasants, or seek to involve the peasants-in-arms who constitute the army; and that failure dragged down with it both the proletariat who were its base, and the enlightened petty bourgeoisie who, in the 'nationalist' government, provided the improvised soviet with but a fragile counterbalance and an ineffective buttress.*

In 1917 as in 1905, Lenin realized that if the urban prole-

*To understand the crucial period of the rise to power of General Torres on 7 October 1970, and the establishment of the Popular Assembly on 1 May 1972, it is helpful to look at the lucid analysis by René Zavaleta, 'Porqué cayó Bolivia en manos del fascismo', *Punto final* (December 1971) – published in English as 'Counter-coup in Bolivia', *New Left Review* (May–June 1972); and at Guillermo Lora's reply, 'Bolivia: De la Asamblea popular al golpe fascista' (April 1972). From

tariat remained isolated from the great mass of the poor and middle peasants, they were doomed to remain impotent. He therefore set the entire policy of the Bolshevik Party, both in peace and in war, towards the magnetic north of a worker–peasant alliance which he called upon everyone to protect 'as the apple of our eye' until his last gasp, even though ready when the time came to give the signal for the strategic retreat represented by the New Economic Policy. Lenin liked quoting Marx's political reflections in this regard, comments that were realistic but read surprisingly from the pen of a man known for his savage scorn for the peasants in theory, as a group who, fragmented or not, represented 'barbarism in the midst of civilization'. Yet Marx also wrote one of the finest and most accurate descriptions of the political reflexes of the peasant class in Bolivia today, after the agrarian reform and the redistribution of land, in *The Eighteenth Brumaire of Louis Bonaparte*. In it he said of France, that predominantly peasant country: 'The proletarian revolution [must obtain] that chorus [i.e. the peasants] without which its solo song in all peasant nations becomes a swan song.' And again, writing to Engels, 16 April 1856: 'The whole thing in

the standpoint we are concerned with here, the situation may be summed up as follows:

The Bolivian proletariat were too mature, too politically demanding, to accept the *de facto* domination of a populist military regime, and to confine their activity within such a framework: hence the establishment of an organ of popular power whose rules demanded that every meeting and every committee must have a majority of workers' votes. But the Bolivian proletariat itself was not strong or resourceful enough to ensure genuine independence for its representative body in relation to the official State system. Thus, when the petty-bourgeois government fell, they were bound to fall too; hence the ease with which Banzer (read Kornilov) could cut off at a single stroke both the petty-bourgeois head and the proletarian head of the popular movement which was itself a single body. For there was one outstanding difference between the Soviet original and its Bolivian reproduction: the Russian soviets included workers, peasants and soldiers side by side, whereas in the Popular Assembly the workers had to all intents and purposes replaced the other two groups – the peasants having only a token representation, and the soldiers none at all.

Germany will depend on the possibility to back the proletarian revolution by some second edition of the Peasants' War. Then the affair will be splendid.'

Scruples, hypotheses and plans of this kind are very much the exception in the Bolivian workers' movement. Whatever aspirations for a 'workers' and peasants' government' may figure in the assemblies and programmes, whatever fine intentions and declarations of principle the trade unions and workers' parties may utter about it, it remains that never at any time has political work among the peasants been taken seriously at national level by the representatives of the working class. In none of their plans of action and publicity, whether political or military, are the peasants – though they are gradually coming to be more differentiated by area, type of country and special interest groups – taken into consideration or expected to contribute anything. The appalling vicious circle spirals steadily downwards: the hypertrophy of the class social consciousness of the proletariat goes hand in hand with the atrophy of the political consciousness of the peasants as an autonomous class; the overdevelopment of trade unionism among industrial workers maintains and reproduces as its opposite the underdevelopment of any real peasant trade unionism; the arrogance of the intellectual petty bourgeoisie towards the working class is exactly paralleled by the arrogance of the working class towards the intellectual bourgeoisie.

I realize that I am giving here a somewhat unfair summing up of a long and complex story. The Bolivian workers' movement is not a static and homogeneous entity, and Trotskyist-inspired attitudes to the national and peasant problem must not be confused with the classical attitudes of communism. The first Latin American Communist Conference, organized in June 1929 by the South American Secretariat of the Third International, started in 1930 a journal, *La Revista communista*. Its first number had this to say of Bolivia after the fall of President Siles:

The workers must begin the struggle for their own demands and against the military junta; the Indians must take up arms and struggle to get back their land – a struggle which can only be effective if it is fought against the government. Fighting councils must be set up among the masses, councils which, as the revolution develops successfully, will be transformed into organs of power. *There is one great danger to the development of the Bolivian revolution: that is that the Indian movements in the countryside will not coincide with the struggle of the workers.* Developing the relationship between the mining proletariat and the Indians is one of the most important objectives we must confront today; only such a bond can provide any guarantee of a determined and powerful movement on the part of the vast mass of the exploited . . .*

These comments certainly give the lie to the reputation for pigheaded dogmatism given to the representatives of the Third International in South America: they display astounding wisdom. But they stand in sharp contrast with what may be called the Founding Charter, and first major theoretical achievement of the Bolivian workers' movement, the Pulacayo Thesis, which I have mentioned. This was produced in 1946 under the inspiration of Guillermo Lora, one of the founders of the Revolutionary Workers' Party (the Fourth International), and it gives only one paragraph to 'the revolutionary collaboration of miners and peasants', at the very end of a national political programme and a general analysis of the tasks of the Bolivian revolution. The 1930 statement made one of the first and most urgent tasks of any future Bolivian Communist Party that 'of ensuring liaison with the Indian population, launching the agrarian revolution and getting large-scale struggles for workers' demands under way'. The Pulacayo Thesis, on the other hand, totally reverses this order of priorities, making union with the peasants appear almost as something remembered only at the last minute.

The twofold isolation of the proletariat: political situation and organizational structure

Let me say again that it would be foolish to suggest that the workers' movement had a deliberate policy of suicide by

* See 'La Revolución derrotada', *La Revista communista*, No. 1, p. 100.

self-isolation. What has happened is a whole historical process independent of the will of the proletarian leaders which was, paradoxically, begun by the 1952 revolution; it has involved the displacement of the various social classes, and changes in their relationships with one another. It is no exaggeration to say that in April 1952 it was the proletariat – represented on that occasion by the industrial workers of La Paz and the miners of Milluni, whose last-minute arrival in La Paz proved decisive in hoisting the *movimientista* petty bourgeoisie (of the MNR) into power. In the early years of the Revolution, it was armed workers who ensured the defence of the government's authority, in the absence of a regular army. The peasants played no part in the April rising, yet it was they who chiefly benefited from the revolution, for its major achievement was the Agrarian Reform. The peasants had their plots of land distributed to them by order of the State, rather than because of any agitation or struggle on their part. Thus the State came to seem to them a miracle-working Father who deserved adoration, distributing land, organizing trade unions for them, and handing out weapons, compensation and cushy jobs to their leaders and deputies. But this filial and religious veneration of the State by the peasants merely served to confirm them in a fundamental misapprehension: they believed that it was the petty bourgeoisie in power behind Paz Estenssoro who had so generously given them the land. In fact it was the proletariat who had brought the MNR to power, and without them he would have fallen in a matter of days; the proletariat was the divine donor. So there gradually came into being a one-sided and exclusive dependence on those who controlled the administration by the beneficiaries of the Agrarian Reform decreed and promulgated by government decision – a decision of which, though they themselves had been the prime instigators, the cost fell most heavily upon the proletariat.

In fact, what the petty bourgeoisie did was simply to colonize the peasants, transform them into its own shock troops and turn them against the proletariat – who thus found themselves an isolated minority, surrounded on all sides and without allies anywhere. Instead of being the reserve army of the revolutionary proletariat, a large proportion of the middle peasant class became the reserve army of the counter-revolutionary bourgeoisie, and of their successors in running the State from 1964 onwards, the armed forces. The famous *Pacto militar-campesino*, ineffective and meaningless as it was, was simply an extension and formalization, by Barrientos and the successive cliques who took his place, of that tacit alliance – automatically formed and automatically renewed – between the successors of the apparent donors of 1952 and the actual beneficiaries, the peasants with their poor scraps of land. As a crowning ingratitude, in the publicity directed by the State to the peasants, the proletariat came to figure as a constant threat; they were supposed to be planning to confiscate land and usurp property with their 'plundering communism', and only the State bureaucracy, actually embodied in the armed forces, stood as a guardian angel between the sinister designs of the 'reds' and the preservation of the gains of the revolution.

The Mexican conjuring-trick achieved perhaps the most utterly incomparable institutional scope and solidity, but at least the Mexican Revolution was genuinely a peasant war, and it seems probable that the peasants there see far enough beyond the omnipotent institutionalized revolutionary party to do justice to themselves and their own magnificent past. But the 1952 Bolivian revolution was a proletarian rising – at least in those decisive days in April – in which the peasant class was conspicuous by its absence; and the proletariat have been ignominiously robbed of their role in history by the ruling civil and military bourgeoisie who now present themselves as the bastion of the peasants' interests. The situation still held in 1967: a class of peasants for the most part passive and non-politicized – except in a few places in the Cochabamba valley where a few enclaves of peasant democracy remained, though isolated and powerless; a retreating petty bourgeoisie, whose political and social organizations were vegetating or quietly dying in the shadow of a State machine totally controlled by the army; and a proletariat ravaged by the 1965 massacres, disarmed, leaderless, starving, friendless, their backs to the wall – the vanguard elements reduced to small-scale underground resistance, and the majority in utter disarray.

In such a situation, the first priority was to break the alliance between the dominant militant bourgeoisie and the dominated peasants. Guerrilla action could and indeed must be part of the response to that political need. 'Here we shall rebuild the alliance between workers and peasants that was broken by anti-popular demagoguery,' declared the ELN's fifth communiqué, written in the hills the day after the St John's Day massacre, and addressed to the miners. This statement highlighted the crucial point at issue.*

The other thing which has up to now prevented the Bolivian proletariat from making the most of its potential reserves of strength, from using them both extensively and intensively for the conquest of political power, is not something extrinsic, accidental or ephemeral, like the social and political isolation we have just been considering, but something intrinsic, structural and permanent. What is a strength

---

* Paradoxically, the guerrillas achieved their aim which was to break down the barriers erected around the working class. But they did not do it as they had expected, through the peasants; the peasants as a class were unaffected by the upheavals of the guerrilla attack. They did it in a quite unexpected way, from the opposite direction, through the democratic petty bourgeoisie in the towns, who were shaken to the core by the repercussions of Guevara's odyssey. As Zavaleta shows clearly in the article I quoted earlier, Ñancahuazú, by whipping up the national consciousness and revolutionary aspirations of all the healthiest, least corrupt elements in the democratic bourgeoisie, both civil and military, brought the working class out of their isolation and gave them a new social ally. By thus giving them political space to move in outside narrow trade-union limits, a platform in the universities, newspaper columns in which to express their demands, and people prepared to present their case favourably to national public opinion, Ñancahuazú indirectly restored the workers' self-confidence.

at one level may well become a weakness when transposed to another. The Bolivian proletariat has developed what is perhaps a unique tendency to amalgamate its awareness of its present economic poverty with its awareness of its future political mission. Its protest against the former and its ambition to carry out the latter converge at the same level, and are seen as achievable through the same means, the trade union – which is understood at once as a shared form of social existence, of political organization and of historical consciousness. The primacy of the trade-union movement over the political vanguard, which has existed for thirty years unquestioned, might be interpreted as an instinctive evasion by the proletariat of its destiny as a 'national class'. This is assuming, of course, that the trade unionism is in this case a revolutionary one, unrelated to the trade unionism of the working-class aristocracies of Europe.

The major documents punctuating the history of the union movement are all political in nature – from the Pulacayo Thesis of 1946, by way of the Colquiri Thesis of 1963, to the Political Thesis adopted at the last COB congress in 1970. The arming of the proletariat, the conquest of power and the establishment of socialism, which do not generally figure among regular trade-union demands elsewhere, are in Bolivia traditional slogans which appear almost automatically. But here it is the form of organization that matters, more than the actual content of what is being demanded. Though the workers' movement is always in danger from economism and reformism, especially in the absence of its most politically aware leaders, and in periods of flux inside the mass movement, it is symptomatic that the political history of the working class is to be found in the development of the confederation of trade unions. Bolivian social struggles have their own peculiar dynamic, whose independence they are determined to preserve. The dynamic of the political struggles develops separately, running parallel to, or at a tangent from, the social, and the two only coincide when there is a revolutionary crisis.

Hence the trade-union organization, however revolutionary the intentions of its members, does not enable the revolutionary energy of the proletariat to acquire that degree of concentration, intensity and convergence of forces required, when the time is ripe, to pierce the armour of the social order and the repressive political machine. The separate development of the social struggle between classes, and the political struggle between parties, is equally harmful to both. The social struggle loses its spearhead and its impact, the political struggle its social base and its in-depth audience. On one side there are large spontaneous and disorganized movements, without leadership or strategic purpose; on the other a proliferation of splinter groups and mini-parties working away in a vacuum of utopian strategy and putting forward endless voluntarist projects which they have no means of carrying out. This divorce is most damaging of all to the interests of the workers. Often and often they have had urgent need of a military arm, but with no political vanguard that the majority of the class could feel any affinity with, they were unable to provide themselves with one. Where there is no political vanguard, there can be no military vanguard that is cohesive, centralized and well-trained enough to fight on all fronts. The trade-union militia, as experience has shown, is incapable either of underground military action, or of any long-term resistance to attack by specialized and better-equipped armed forces. If any lessons are to be drawn from history, then this would seem to be the lesson of the present-day history of political and social struggle in Bolivia: outside the workers' movement, and apart from the trade-union organization which is its mass embodiment, no revolutionary transformation seems possible. But inside the workers' movement alone, having regard solely to the only methods of struggle directly accessible to it, no revolutionary transformation is possible either. These two negative statements may help us to mark out our position. A definite field of action is delimited by these two negative boundaries. But that field of action can only be of value to a Bolivian political vanguard whose objective is to gain power. It certainly does not exclude a guerrilla war, provided the vanguard that launches that war has one foot solidly in the workers' and semi-proletarian movement, either directly, or indirectly by means of alliances and coordination with friendly political elements.

The military equations:
  Leading force without rank and file = *vanguard without rear-guard* = *offensive without defensive* = *attack with nowhere to fall back to*

This apparent detour was in fact necessary: one must examine class relationships in Bolivia if one is to get to the heart of our subject – relationships of power. The latter are the translation into military terms of the former. The course of Bolivian history is so marked, even in its narrowest by-ways, by the use of violence, that the over-quoted phrase of Clausewitz can only be applied to it if it is turned on its head: in Bolivia, politics is the continuation of civil war by other means. There is no class, party or caste that does not at all times impose its will on its opponents by means of force, or that variant of force which is political chicanery.

As we have seen, the class which is in the majority, but scattered over too wide a territory and without any internal cohesion, has appeared on the social scene as, so to say, a negative class, whose unrest and revolt have made no impact at the political level. On the other hand, the tiny minority of the proletariat have been so concentrated as to be able to control the possibilities for political action by all those exploited by private or State capital. We can thus see how, in a country whose population is two-thirds *rural*, any way in which political conflict can be violently resolved is totally *urban*, in its every phase. Revolutionary action begins in the town, and almost at once reaches its apogee there. Whether it is transferring the State power from a civilian to a military group, from one military group to another, or from one class to another, every change in Bolivian political history looks like a 180-degree turn, violent and unexpected, but decisive. 9 April 1952, 4

November 1964, 7 October 1970, 23 August 1971: the events of the class struggle all take the classic form of 'the day of the revolution', whether successful or not. In that respect they are more like the annals of the French or Russian revolution than the Chinese or Vietnamese, whose 'campaigns' are dated by the season or even the year.

These social spasms end in a few hours either with complete defeat or complete victory; and when it is defeat, the popular attacking forces can only go into hiding or exile, or be disbanded. They produce the fusion of two opposing lightning-flash actions – that of the military '*coup*', and that of the 'popular uprising'; for in the final analysis, a direct confrontation clears away all the inessentials of class relationship, and brings to grips the only two forces which are really decisive in society, the armed forces on the one side, and the working class on the other. All other sectors are either peripheral to what is happening, or destroyed by it; and though they may well have a vote in peacetime, they can claim no right to be heard in these laconic and decisive moments which provide a kind of instant X-ray of the body of society, and make clear what it is really like. Thus each of the two sides tries to be the fastest to act, for it goes without saying that the first to arrive at the gates of the Palacio Quemado (the presidential palace in La Paz) will sit in the presidential chair, and stay sitting there, at least until the next *coup*. Obviously the army is better equipped to win this race for time. However, on 9 April 1952, the 'ordinary people' of La Paz, reinforced by the nearest mineworkers, managed to get to the finishing line before the MNR's military conspirators; they had not foreseen this upsurge of the populace in arms, and the revolution was a success.

On 4 November 1964, on the other hand, the military conspiracy got there first, and slammed the gates of the presidential palace in the faces of the same armed populace, to produce a counter-revolution. In factual terms: when Juan Lechín was borne in triumph on the shoulders of his supporters to the main gate of the Palacio Quemado, it was already occupied by the army, and machine-gun fire, mowing down the demonstrators in the Plaza Murillo, forced the crowd to disperse.

In short, though the military *coup* is the classic form of the change-over of power among the various ruling factions, 'the transformation of the *coup d'état* into a popular uprising' is an undeniable historic experience; and on that the traditional populist forces rely both as a rallying-cry to the masses, and as their preferred means of action, which is a civil-cum-military conspiracy. It is not hard to imagine what putchist and opportunist temptations can attach to such an endeavour, when the planned *coup* is simply carried out from above, independent of any mobilization of the masses along class lines. In any case what is not a historical experience, and cannot be made a credible and effective rallying-cry, is the transformation of a failed popular rising into a long-term revolutionary civil war. Why not?

As we have seen, the history of class relations in Bolivia is the history of a leading class which, in the absence of a main force to lead, must itself also be the main force. We can thus understand why the history of attacks by the dominated classes on the militarily fortified ruling classes is the history of assaults by a front-line vanguard – without any rearguard or, often, even any central core – against the walls of a military fortress. Should the first wave of the attack manage to dislodge the enemy, by surprise, or through sheer impetus, then the fortress will fall or surrender, and the day is won. But if the first wave is repulsed, for lack of adequate weapons, coordination or speed, then, despite all their enthusiasm and spirit of sacrifice, those behind fall back in disorder and confusion, with no proper plan of retreat, and the day is lost. Since there is no social force to support them and protect their flank, take over from them, bring reinforcements and supplies to those of the proletarian force who are in the front line, there is no relief force for a second wave of attack, no position prepared to fall back to in an organized retreat. So there is never a 'second wind' in the attack. When the front line retreats, it becomes every man for himself among those behind. Lack of coordination results in total rout. The verdict of failure is final; the case is settled with no possibility of appeal. Without a rearguard support base the insurgents have no logistical resources for fighting on, nor that 'politico-moral stimulation' which both Stalin and Giap have declared essential to any fighting front. The uprising cannot develop into a war of movement, still less of course a war from entrenched positions. The attrition is all on one side – it is the insurgents in the streets around the garrisons, or beneath the walls of the Miraflores Headquarters, who are worn down, not the military machine. In short, the slow and gradual encircling of the towns from the country areas (that universal model so beloved of the late Lin Piao) has never, for objective and unanswerable reasons, become a feature of the Bolivian scene, despite the preponderantly rural population. Since the death of Túpaj Katarí, the art of the siege has vanished from the military skills of the Bolivian people.

It is the relations existing among the various classes, then, that determine the disposition of the available forces. The weak point in that disposition is always and obviously the same: its inability to cope with even the slightest, briefest setback. There must be immediate and total success; it cannot survive the most minor blow from the enemy, for partial failure means total defeat. A simple tactical reverse limited by the time and place of the armed confrontation becomes a strategic disaster over the entire territory, at every level of social development and for a long period of time. The smallest weak point in the conspiracy, the smallest imponderable in a spontaneous uprising, can take on the dimensions of a crucial event on which victory or defeat hinges totally.*

* For example: on 23 August 1971 in La Paz, an unforeseen hitch, like the arrival at the gates of the General Headquarters, of three armoured machine-gun carriers, which had got through the vigilance of the people by appearing to come in support of the established Torres government only a few minutes before it was attacked by armed civilians, was enough to determine the whole outcome. The civilians who had found bazookas

Hence we can see how the common sense of the Bolivian people, long accustomed to this sort of sudden and dramatic change, and to suffering the consequences with stoic fatalism, runs clean counter to the historical common sense whereby, to recall Clausewitz, 'no State' – and, we may add, no class, no party – 'must ever accept that its fate, that is its existence, depends on a single battle, however decisive'. This paradox is a commonplace in Bolivia, where arming the people is not a utopian dream but a regular development; and its effects similarly contradict, almost word for word, Clausewitz's Chapter 26 on 'The Arming of the People' – though what he says is quite valid in relation to the historical experiences of his time. In fact, the Bolivian people's war in no way corresponds to the conditions laid down by that excellent author at the beginning of the last

---

and ammunition on the hill of Laikakota which they captured from the army, did not know how to use them, and the soldiers of Major Rubén Sánchez's battalion had used up their reserves of ammunition. In purely technical terms (and therefore unrelated to the dominant political context), it was that minuscule tactical incident which enabled Brazil to win what was to all intents and purposes a common frontier with Chile; Brazil was now in a position to organize a constant infiltration of arms, men and equipment to the rearguard position of Chilean fascism, to say nothing, of course, of the establishment in Bolivia itself of a fascist regime unparalleled in its history. Certainly no 'war for political conquest' in Latin America was ever more lightly and cheaply won.

The continental significance of that local episode seems to have escaped the protagonists, but certainly did not escape its American stage manager. That day in August 1971 marked an about-face all over the continent, with the initiative passing from the anti-imperialist camp to the enemy, the end of one stage and the beginning of another from which we have not yet emerged. It is common for the historical significance of their own victories and defeats to escape both victors and vanquished at the time of fighting. Perhaps that is providential: to grasp the meaning and the consequences of what they are doing might well inhibit both their speech and their action. Lenin who, with the understanding of history outlined by Marx, worked out and put to the test a science of politics, did not find it hard to understand what was 'historic' about his political experience; he made a simultaneous translation, so to say, from day to day, of his political statements into the language of history. But Lenin is merely the exception that proves the rule. He engendered no such ability in those who have come after him.

century (and still by no means out of date, to judge by such modern readers as Lenin, Che and Mao). He says in that same chapter:

The only conditions that can make a popular war effective are the following:
1. The war must be drawn out to the countryside.
2. A single disaster must not be enough to settle it.
3. The theatre of the fighting must cover a considerable part of the territory.
4. The action taken must be suited to the national character.
5. The country must be cut off or inaccessible, either because it is mountain or swampland or forest, or because of its specific culture.

In Bolivia the situation is such that only the fourth condition is met. Unfortunately the national character of the measures taken up to now has consisted in systematically going against all the other conditions – an artful way of interpreting texts in social practice not envisaged by Clausewitz! As we know from Goethe, the tree of life is always greener than the stunted bushes of theory. However, the restricted nature of the theatre of operations in most Bolivian civil wars has more than once proved disastrous, by making it impossible to establish the firmly based defence system that is the key to any long-term national resistance. The impetus and enthusiasm which mark urban revolutionary operations can only be replaced by tenacity and coolheadedness if there is a corresponding change of method and scene. Clearly, then, the alliance between workers and peasants must be at the core of the armed revolution in Bolivia, for only the combination of the crucial urban sectors with the rural sectors needed for prolonged resistance can make it possible for an armed rising in the capital to spread outwards; the initial nucleus must expand and merge into a different and wider area where they could be hidden, encouraged and supported, given shelter, food, and so on.

But how bridge the gulf between the popular revolutionary outburst, that national, traditional method of resolving basic class conflicts – which, though undoubtedly recognized by the masses as historically legitimate, is precarious, sporadic and exposed to reverses and setbacks – and a national war of resistance fought at the grass roots and over a long period, which is the complete and typical form taken by all the successful guerrilla wars in the world today? There does really seem to be a gap, a difference of approach, an enormous gulf to be bridged between the two, in view of the unfriendly, desert terrain of the altiplano, the apathy of the Indians living outside the large towns, and the insurgents' lack of both equipment and transport. And this is not just a hypothetical problem, but one which has several times presented itself as an urgent matter requiring a here-and-now solution.

In his book *Diez meses de emergencia en Bolivia*, Jorge Gallardo, Minister of the Interior in the Torres government, tells the story of how he suggested to General Torres at the end of August 1971 that the armed civilians, with the few troops who remained loyal, should withdraw from La Paz towards the Alto Beni (a tropical area at a lower level than the capital and only some few dozen kilometres away) so as to be able to carry on the fight in better conditions. It was by no means an unrealistic plan: the prevailing geographical and social conditions would certainly have made it possible to undertake it. But it was not tried because of General Torres's declared fear that they would be bombarded from the air en route. It was in fact obvious that his heart was not in it. A similar movement could equally have taken place from the town of Cochabamba to the near-by region of Chapare, and several of the ELN leaders intended at one time to attempt it; but that plan was never carried out either.

The reason why plans of this kind have never actually been adopted is not hard to discover. Che had pointed it out four years earlier, when he made it clear to Mario Monje that you cannot in a day improvise a withdrawal from the city to a guerrilla base in the country. It was just this problem of the link between the urban revolt and rural guerrilla force which had been one of the objections made

by Monje to Guevara – and earlier, in 1966, by several of
the communist leadership to Papi and Pombo, when they
were making ready to receive Che in La Paz. Obviously in
this particular situation, those using this argument were in
fact using it as a political alibi. In itself it demanded serious
consideration, but the then leadership of the CP managed
ingeniously to prejudge the question, and to confuse content
with method. The fact that there must be a link between
the urban and rural movements does not mean that the
work of establishing guerrilla groups in the country cannot
start until there has been an urban uprising, or even that
no guerrilla fighting should begin until there has been a
political crisis in the city. A revolt cannot be planned or
carried out to order; but a guerrilla operation must be
planned and prepared in advance. A guerrilla operation
cannot be an improvised coming-together of those who have
survived a defeat, civilians in a state of rout, cold and foot-
sore, without purpose or leadership, without any prepared
support or supplies, without any previous knowledge of the
terrain and with no communications system. This was what
Che said to Monje at Christmas 1966, when Monje said
that guerrilla warfare in Bolivia must be the direct follow-
up of an uprising. To Che it was out of the question to make
the whole issue, the undertaking of a struggle that must last
for several years, depend on a few hours of fighting. Though
the objective was right and there was a certain basis for it
in Bolivian history, the argument was, in this form, wholly
unacceptable. The setting up and taking root of a guerrilla
movement could not depend on the unpredictable and by
definition undefined organization of a generalized revolt in
the capital. What the Party leadership was in fact doing, by
making 'combination' (that ideally the two should take
place simultaneously) mean 'subordination' (*first* the urban
revolt, *then* the guerrilla movement), was trying to evade,
delay, and ultimately put off indefinitely the guerrilla war
directed by Che.

4

Che's Strategy

In any case, no analysis of the sort we have been making, restricted to the here-and-now situation in Bolivia, would invalidate Che's plans. The most it could do would be to question whether it was tactically possible for a guerrilla *foco* to overcome the problems involved in taking root in the countryside in its first phase. And Che, whose thinking was always more that of a strategist than a tactician, would have no reason to submit to, or be restrained by, its conclusions. The simple reason is that Che's strategy did not have Bolivia as its target – nor even as its *prime* objective. Indeed, all these considerations would be compelling only within the closed framework of the national territory of Bolivia, only if his furthest horizon were the takeover of power in Bolivia. In that country, as we have seen, the shortest road to gaining power does not lie through the countryside, and certainly does not start from a semi-desert rural area – if only because the peasant class, especially since the Agrarian Reform, are not the moving force for revolution in Bolivia.

Having said that, what next? What point is there in our argument if the objective of Ñancahuazú was not the town of La Paz at all? By choosing a theatre of operations so distant geographically from the centres of political power, Che was really making it clear that he was opting for a different field of history. By keeping his distance, in every sense, from Bolivia's political struggles and the terrain upon which they were normally fought – urban insurrection allied with military conspiracy – he was pushing away the horizon, so to say, from what he saw as a provincial objective: if Latin America was the *Patria grande* waiting to come to birth, then the small *patrias* within it could never be more than provinces.

Further: not merely was such a continental strategy something unique, at least in our century, in its sheer size; it was even more so in its content and method. That was Che's radical innovation. At the same time as extending his field of vision beyond national boundaries to the whole continent, he also turned the traditional methods of action of the revolutionary 'left' completely upside down, an astounding thing to do, especially in Latin America. For in fact, Che's immediate objective was not to seize power, but first of all to build up a popular power with its own effective organ of activity, an autonomous and mobile military force. In his view, the establishment of a popular power took precedence over the seizure of power in Bolivia, which came second both in time and in importance. This reversal of the order of historical factors and episodes represented a definite break with local tradition (indeed it may have been *too* revolutionary a break, too ambitious, too sharp, given the precarious conditions and the modest resources available to him in the local political climate). The normal thing in Latin America is *first* to take over the power of the State, the existing bureaucratic and military system; then, *afterwards*, a 'progressive' or 'populist' government, acting from above, and using that bourgeois power as a lever, will try to lay the foundations for popular power.

In Bolivia this 'before' and 'after' have tended to be so telescoped as to occur simultaneously in the form of a seemingly dual power (the COB/MNR in 1952, the Popular Assembly/Torres government in 1971); but even then, the popular power, though having its own distinct social content, has no specific political substance, because the organs of that popular power have never been created on autonomous foundations independent of – in other words *antedating* – the organs of power of the bourgeois State. In this sense, Che was undoubtedly breaking with the 'putschist' customs and the propensity to *pronunciamientos* of present-day populism, both in Bolivia and elsewhere, but he did so to get back to the basic teaching of Marx that the proletarian revolution 'cannot simply take over a ready-made State machine, but must destroy the military and bureaucratic machine of the bourgeois State, and establish the dictatorship of the proletariat'.

This somewhat disconcerting rediscovery of the purest theoretical tradition of revolutionary Marxism, which had been distorted or overlaid by decades of opportunist routine, had a direct practical consequence. To put it at its most superficial: when Che started a revolution in Bolivia he was not presenting himself as a candidate for the presidency, nor were the guerrillas seeking ministerial office. In this sense, the reservations and sensibilities of the popular national leaders towards the guerrilla war, and the panic of the regular officers suddenly faced with the prospect of being driven out of their cushy bureaucratic jobs, resulted from a total misapprehension. Che was not in competition with either group: not from any moral purism, but mainly for reasons of effectiveness in terms of his own political and military strategy.

Neither in the short term nor the long was the seizure of power in La Paz ever the objective of Ñancahuazú. Indeed to Che it would have been a real catastrophe if circumstances should have so precipitated matters that a premature victory cut short his plan for history: a plan which could only bear fruit in the fullness of time, by delaying its effects for as long as possible. A popular regime in Bolivia, with himself directly or indirectly in control, would have been a millstone round his neck. In the then international situation (without Velasco Alvarado in Peru, or Allende in Chile) it would have meant complete encirclement and an economic blockade. A socialist economy reduced to autarchy in the landlocked situation of Bolivia, with no exit to the sea, with no blast-furnaces for its ore, no sure market for its oil, no home-produced flour for its bread, would not, in Che's eyes, have been viable. At that stage he was not concerned with State responsibilities, for they would only have prevented his long-term plan from achieving fulfilment, and led into a deceptively attractive dead-end the Long March which could alone reach the real objective: the slow bringing to birth of a Latin American political-cum-military vanguard, or, more precisely, the establishment of a seed-bed of national vanguards which would, bit by bit, spread over all the countries on the continent. This called for time and patience, and from those involved, for a certain spirit of sacrifice as regards their immediate political wishes. It would not have been wise to get too close to the towns, or to make it a tactical objective to enter urban centres, for that vanguard, with the form and membership of a guerrilla troop, that is to say of a mobile strategic force, could only grow and become established by developing in the country-side. Thus in the first phase, Bolivia could not and should not be anything more than the ground where the central seed must be implanted and must grow, and gradually come to spread outwards by natural division.

What Che's full plans were has never, at least to my knowledge, been put into writing – far less published. He never even formulated them explicitly or systematically at any time to the guerrilla band at Ñancahuazú. Those plans were omnipresent, but unspoken, guessed by most of them, glimpsed more fully by others, and known only to a small number. Yet only in their light can we understand fully the first acts in the guerrilla war, his dialogue with the CP, his refusal to let Monje take over the political leadership of the guerrilla war; even the ultimate choice of that spot in south-east Bolivia as the place to establish the guerrilla war can only be understood in the light of those plans. Yet to the very end it remained a light interspersed with shadow. Why was that? Undoubtedly there were technical reasons, due to the way the work was compartmentalized. Who, apart from Fidel and Che, could have outlined the precise con-tours of that vast historical project secretly being worked out in so many hearts, and a few heads too, in the middle sixties (say the time between the Tricontinental and OLAS con-ferences)? And who today, apart from Fidel and his closest collaborators, could retrace that outline faithfully?

Yet it is hard not to think that Che had other reasons for

maintaining a reserve about the future at that particular time and place: he may well have felt a certain reluctance, almost embarrassment, at the idea of painting a canvas whose vast scope must have seemed so ludicrously out of proportion to the precariousness of the situation and the all too inadequate means then at his disposal. To express ambition on such a scale might well have given more discouragement than exaltation to the participants, at a time when the obstacles to be overcome, the successive stages to be gone through, the gaps to be filled between the present and the future, the real and the imaginary, the means available and the end in view, appeared so uncertain, so difficult, so enormous. How could fifty or so guerrillas in an isolated country area make it their goal to bring total liberation to a continent with nearly 300 million people in it, without losing something of their modesty and certainly their lightheartedness? I should say that only those who have studied the historical paradoxes surrounding the beginnings of Latin America, who remember how a handful of men under Pizarro and Cortez first conquered America, and another handful under Bolívar and San Martín later liberated half of it, can realize how unwise it is to ridicule such an ambition, at least in principle. In 1967, that ambition, disproportionate and grandiose though it may have seemed, was not yet a plan worked out in diagram, not yet a defined and detailed programme – but neither was it a spur-of-the-moment dream, or a vague Utopia built of words alone. It was perhaps half way between the two – what may be called a 'project'. It existed as a series of vistas and dotted lines, but its main features were already visible to the naked eye on the political map of the continent. Let us look at it more closely.

Whether consciously or not, Che, who had always talked of the day when 'the Andes would become the Sierra Maestra of America', saw that future somewhat in terms of the past, of his own experience in Cuba. In this sense, his vision was transposing onto a continental scale the experience of the original column in the Sierra Maestra (though not as a mechanical repetition of it); that column, as it developed, produced off-shoots, separate columns which grew in their turn, and moved away to open other fronts until the entire territory was covered. That paradigm experience of the rebel army certainly provided Che with an implicit model from the point of view of military practice. The inherent advantages in this type of organic development have often been pointed out: strategic centralization and tactical decentralization, unity of purpose and diversity in ways of carrying it out, the natural subordination of every group to its mother-group together with the autonomy of each individual guerrilla force. This is what I wrote in 1966 in *Revolution in the Revolution?*:

The advantage of this progression from smaller to larger, which is deceptively simple and apparently effortless, is that it proclaims the simultaneous existence of an undisputed central command and a very great tactical freedom for its officers and columns. The stronger the central command and the more lucid and firm its strategy from the start, the greater will be the freedom of action and the tactical flexibility of its various fronts and columns. The concentration of resources and men in a single *foco* permits the elaboration of a single military doctrine, in the heat of the combats in which the men receive their training . . . Thus, little by little, officers are formed in a certain moral, political, and military school, officers in whom the high command, when the day comes, can confidently place the strategic leadership of a zone or front, without the need to control their actions. They are all trained together, in the same school, which inculcates in them a common spirit, tactical rules, and a step-by-step political and military plan of action.*

When Fidel's column had reached its maximum size for the resources of the area and the demands of mobility, Raul's column broke away from it early in 1957, to go and open the second front in the north of Oriente province; then came Almeida's column in the area around Santiago in March 1957; then in August 1958, the columns of Che and

* *Revolution in the Revolution?* (Penguin, 1966), pp. 79-80.

Camilo moved towards Las Villas. In the same sort of way, when the Ñancahuazú column became large enough, a smaller column would break away and move to the second front north of Cochabamba, then another to open the third front in the Alto Beni, north of La Paz (the leaders of both were already appointed within the group, though their names were not publicly announced). These three connected fronts were to constitute the central Bolivian *foco*. At a later stage, further columns would move outwards from it to other countries. One would go to Peru, its kernel consisting of the Peruvian comrades now in the original column, and would join up with a guerrilla base already established in Ayacucho province in south-west Peru. Another column would move to Argentina, this one composed of a majority of Argentinians; it would certainly be larger than the Peruvian one, and obviously when the time came Che himself would lead it. It is important to remember that after Cuba, Argentina was Che's most beloved 'homeland', the dream that went with him all his life, and quite possibly the secret goal of all his activities.

Other countries would all come in their turn. The Bolivian *foco* would then function as a military training centre and political coordinating centre for all the other national revolutionary organizations of the continent. The individuals with greatest potential from each country would be brought there and temporarily incorporated into Che's Bolivian *foco*, from which they would return to their national bases as trained politico-military cadres. In this way Che's original guerrilla group would multiply by natural reproduction till it extended over the continent. The ideal to which Che's action was directed, and which we may use as an intermediate schema between the situation as it then was and the dynamic project being brought to achievement, might be described thus: an international network, at once homogeneous and flexible, covering the whole of Latin America, made up of national politico-military organizations. Those organizations would have the same basic structure – of guerrilla armies; identical initials –

ELN (Army of National Liberation); a single theory of war – that of Che and the politically united group gathered round him; and a political vision on a world scale. Che's own column would be the centre of that network.

Only Che could establish and set in motion so grandiose a project, and it would take years, even perhaps decades. We may judge it to have been premature, but it had a solid enough historical and political basis to make it quite realistic. The earlier days of the First Independence lent it a certain mythical power to arouse people, at the same time as undeniable historical authenticity: Bolívar acted in just the same way at Angostura. The men who fought for the First Independence were also international columns, predominantly Latin American, constituting a central trunk from which the various armies of liberation developed like so many branches.

But what Che was principally relying upon was a developing situation. His network was not going to be formed solely out of its centre in Bolivia, but from several simultaneous developments; in many cases all that his forces had to do was to get together, if not physically at least politically, with guerrilla fronts and forces already in existence in outlying areas but needing reinforcement or coordination. It was this fact that made his plan a real political vision and not just a chimera. The workers, materials, and tools were all there: all that remained to be done was to bring together the scattered pieces, put them under one roof, give an already ongoing enterprise a common aim, a unified leadership, a constructional cohesion. In this sense, Che was not so much the architect of something that had to be built up from scratch, as a contractor taking over the construction of an edifice already under way, with whole sections already completed.

In Guatemala, Turcios had died early in October 1966, but the FAR (Revolutionary Armed Forces) still had 300 men under arms at the end of the year in Izabal and Zacapa provinces. When Che arrived in Bolivia, Arana Osorio's military attack on the Guatemalan guerrillas had not yet been successful.

In Venezuela, in the Yaracuy and Falcón mountains, the recovery plan I have spoken of had taken shape at that same time, and a large column of guerrillas, strengthened by the 1966 landing – and not all the expected landings had taken place – seemed to have every hope for the future.

In Colombia there was the ELN *foco* led by Fabio Vásquez in Santander, and other guerrilla forces which might be more or less useful.

In Peru the ELN was on its way to reorganization, which is why some of its militants were already in Ñancahuazú – Jose Cabrera Flores (el Negro), for instance, and Lucio Galván (Eustaquio). Juan Pablo Chang (el Chino) was responsible for communications with the forces inside Peru, and for coordinating the establishment of a further front that was about to come into action, with which liaison must later be made.

In Argentina, Che had depended from the first on the remainder of the EGP and its previous infrastructure, as well as on the embryo revolutionary left now humming with activity: Che's guerrilla plans there gave birth, whether directly or indirectly, to the FAR and the PCR (Revolutionary Communist Party), which broke away at that time from the Argentinian Young Communist League.

Contacts with Brazil were by way of certain 'nationalist revolutionary' forces, mainly composed of former soldiers, sailors and NCOs grouped in the south of Brazil around a popular leader. On the borders of Minas Gerais and Espírito Santo, that movement was establishing the bases of a rural guerrilla *foco*, in the Caparao mountains; but the *foco* was discovered in its training stage and disbanded by a battalion of the First Brazilian Army, in April 1967, just as Che was starting to make contact. The expected coordination therefore never occurred. The dissident groups in the Brazilian CP had not yet become organized or even visible, and though Marighela had come onto the scene and begun to express his ideas at the end of 1966, the Brazilian ALN did not yet exist. There could therefore be no organic contact with the forces which later emerged to launch the urban guerrilla war in Brazil in 1968. Che, however, informed of Marighela's preparations – at that stage only intentions – late in the day, took care to include the situation prevailing in the regional committee of the CP in São Paulo among the matters on which I was to report back to him later on, when I returned.

As for Che's stop in Montevideo before coming to Bolivia, that belongs to the realm of those undying myths destined for the innumerable journalists of revolutionary folklore who find themselves short of copy. At that moment, Che only had indirect links with Uruguay, and not through the Tupamaros. At the end of 1966 they were only a tiny, isolated group, almost without infrastructure, and with no international relations worthy of the title; indeed it was on 22 December of that year that the organization had its first brush with the police, accidental and premature, in which Carlos Flores and Mario Robaina died – one of the worst moments in all the ups and downs of the movement. I myself never once heard Che mention the existence of the Tupamaros or any urban guerrilla organization in Uruguay. Of course Uruguay figured in Che's plans, but indirectly, and through the intermediary of Uruguayans outside their country. But all that was envisaged was the later incorporation of a young organization whose best-known leader was simply a nationalist. The Eastern Revolutionary Movement (MRO), discounting any possibility of armed struggle in the towns, adopted at that date the then accepted criteria for guerrilla war – that it should be both rural and on a continental scale. Hence the members of the MRO thought it their first duty to leave their country and join the continental army being formed outside it. The Tupamaros, as we know, did not share this view, and despite all the risks involved in staying, refused to leave Uruguay, and maintained against all comers that there was a definite place and sure future for the armed struggle.*

* In this connection I should like to recall one highly significant anecdote which has over the years gained semi-public notoriety. Several Tupamaro leaders have described how their small group, then in a very

Che's enterprise was thus a kind of hinge-point between the past and the future. Though appearing as the crest of one wave of history, it also represented the supreme test of actually putting into practice a certain concept of the armed struggle which had been developed and defined in his written works in the early sixties, and was now being realized in various parts of Latin America under the combined influence, and at the instigation, of Fidel and himself. It was the focal point of a number of existing guerrilla organizations and of half-formed, partially executed plans all over the continent; thus it represented both the synthesis, the attempt to create a totality out of a whole period of fairly developed struggles, and their elevation to a higher level of military organization and political planning.

But one can say more. It was as though Fidel and Che realized intuitively that if they could not get to that higher level, if they failed to become unified and coordinated, the

---

difficult position, received a proposal from the leadership of the Uruguayan CP that they take part in a continental guerrilla war outside the country. It is also recalled that, at that same moment, the Cuban revolution received an offer from the leadership of the Uruguayan CP to send a certain number of Uruguayan revolutionaries who were in difficulties to join Che's guerrilla group. There is nothing specially surprising about that: the Uruguayan CP admit quite openly the validity, and indeed long-term inevitability, of the armed struggle in a great many Latin American countries, and Uruguay in particular, though they do see it in strategic rather than tactical terms. There is no secret about any of this, and it was on this basis that the Secretary General, Rodney Arismendi, played such a positive and outstanding role at the OLAS conference of August 1967. What does, however, remain in some doubt is whether by thus, unasked, playing the part of benevolent intermediary between the Tupamaros and Che's guerrilla group, the CP was proving its genuine solicitude and international solidarity, or merely making a skilful manoeuvre to rid Uruguay of the budding revolutionary organization known as the Tupamaros. In any case, Uruguay did play a certain part in the preparations of Ñancahuazú, though it was somewhat by chance: it was in fact during the Uruguayan CP's congress in August 1966 that Kolle, then a member of the secretariat of the Bolivian CP, informed the leadership of the Uruguayan Party that there was a guerrilla plan directed towards the 'southern cone', in which Cubans were playing a predominant part.

struggles in progress would inevitably lose their impetus, sink back into themselves and eventually become dispersed, being restricted and stifled in and by their own national or even regional, party or even sectarian, boundaries. Either those boundaries must be overcome by synthesis, or the various isolated struggles would collapse of themselves. Either the guerrilla groups of the time must at last work together for a coherent political plan on a continental scale, or they were doomed to bleed to death, each dying alone from its own internal haemorrhage, and nothing could save them. The Cuban revolution was obviously a vital party in this hoped-for synthesis. The direction and meaning of the whole Latin American guerrilla war could not be isolated from the ultimate direction and meaning of the Cuban revolution.

The experiences and fighting-weapons accumulated up to then by the guerrillas in Latin America were such as to make it possible for a plan like Che's to be developed for the future. But all these other endeavours depended in their turn on the execution of that plan. They looked to it for their own salvation – both their present physical safety and their ultimate success – and it was that success that Che had determined to achieve without delay, come what may. We can see what was involved: for the whole of a certain period, the rural guerrilla war in Latin America was, so to say, staking its last farthing. This form of revolutionary war was to become the 'summation' of that period of history – the horizon circumscribing all its vicissitudes – the moment when it shattered into a thousand fragments, mortally wounded, to give way to a new concept, new methods, new protagonists: in other words, to a new period.

The 'events' of history are linked together in spirals, one connecting up with the next in alternating curves. Each arc of a circle represents a distinct 'period', and at a given moment all these curves reach a point in their bend which marks the 'transition' from one period to the next. Ñanca-huazú was undoubtedly the highest curve in the course of one part of Latin American revolutionary history. The question is whether the summit it touched was the rise after a period of decline, or the fall after a period of ascent. Was it the crowning point or the end of ten years of scattered guerrilla fighting? Was it a zenith or a heroic death? The end of one era or the beginning of another? For every trajectory has its peak, after which the projectile starts its downward journey.

In short, a great many questions depend on the answer to the first one: what was the relationship of the past history of the guerrilla war to Ñancahuazú? What effect did Che's action have on the course of political history? And what repercussions did the Cuban revolution have on the continental revolution, given that whatever form it may have led it to take must in turn have determined the place of the Cuban revolution on the international scene. For everything is interconnected.

If any single project in the present-day history of South America deserves to be called 'crucial', it is what Che stood for in those doubtful, undecided, foggy days of the southern winter in 1967. At no moment in modern Latin America has the fate of so many people depended on such a tiny handful of men. All the revolutionaries all over the continent – both those in arms and those placing their hope in legal means, those in positions of power and responsibility in Cuba, as well as those still fighting to win power everywhere else – all of them were unconsciously being summoned to the 'court' of that isolated forest to hear what role would be attributed to each in the drama of Latin America today. Or perhaps to what political choice they would find themselves impelled on the national and international scene. At the time, of course, they were completely unaware of what was happening. The decision was made in their absence, by default if you like. But did they even understand afterwards what they had brought upon themselves?

The leaders of the Cuban revolution were, in fact, the only ones to understand all that was at issue. They could not fail to understand the full scope of the enterprise, just as they could not help sooner or later forming certain conclusions from its results. For they were supremely implicated in that global historic project, since it was theirs as well: they were physically present, politically responsible, and morally committed. Since politics is, for want of a better definition, the art of the possible, there are policies which are possible in theory but which a modification in the balance of forces can render impossible in practice, whether one likes it or not. Certainly the Cuban revolution explored every possibility to the full – to the limit of its forces and beyond. And surely it was Che's involvement with that revolution, its past and its future, which drove him to throw himself into this irrevocable, absolute, final commitment. I am convinced that, had his national responsibilities left him free to do so, Fidel would gladly have committed himself personally as well.

5

Choice of Terrain

THIS creeping insurrection that was to put out branches all over a continent was still, at the beginning of 1967, no more than a seedling, or perhaps rather a cutting that might or might not 'take'. You cannot plant out just any plant at any time of year in any sort of soil. To grow, it must first take root; therefore the major need is to find the right soil for establishing and nourishing a guerrilla force. The feebleness of the existing resources need not cast doubt on the viability of the enterprise: after all a foetus looks the same whether it is going to miscarry, or grow into a large and healthy child. The only condition that must be recognized as utterly indispensable for the building up of a strong vanguard is a stable rearguard. The highest oak-tree is only as strong as its roots underground.

If Bolivia was ultimately to be transformed into one huge support base, the first thing to be done was to find a suitable place in Bolivia to set up a guerrilla mini-base. Since quick action in emergencies could be decisive, everything depended on the guerrilla group's capacity for coping with the various precarious elements of functioning underground. In this sense, the problem on which Che's entire strategy depended was that of choosing the zone of operations where the guerrilla troop could grow and survive most naturally. At the planning stage of a series of actions, any last-minute change of direction, any slight error of vision, any hitch in selecting the time and place for starting operations, would inevitably have a quite disproportionate repercussion at a later stage. That is why it is so well worth examining all the details of the preparatory phase under a magnifying glass; by seeing them ten times their size one can form a precise picture of the proper scale of their long-term effects, which it would otherwise be hard to see with the naked eye.

Unfortunately, however, guerrilla warfare has little in common with horticulture. Che's preparations were subject to all the chaos, the hazards and the uncertainties of underground work, especially in a soil as liable to upheavals as Bolivia, and they did not, in their first phase, get exactly the loving care of the nursery gardener. And though it is true that the time and place of the start of the armed struggle turned out to be cruelly unfavourable, it is also true that the choice of that time and place was to a large extent outside the control of the leadership and of Che himself.

The choice of terrain was obviously the most vital problem. This was, in my view, so unfortunate that, though not the determining cause of the failure, it was a decisive factor in producing the difficulties encountered by the guerrilla force from the first. For such a force not to be free to decide on its own moment for entering into action, for it to be in danger of having to make a premature move, or of being forced by an enemy initiative to come into the open before it has completed its groundwork – anything of that kind inescapably brings into play a number of imponderables, of unforeseeable things which one should, in theory, somehow be able to have foreseen. More than one prematurely discovered guerrilla force has succeeded in escaping liquidation, as for instance in Cuba, when eighty expeditionaries from the *Granma* landed at Niquero in Oriente province. But if the first nucleus of fighters are discovered and surrounded, on ground unsuited to any prolonged resistance or even to the logistical survival of a small guerrilla group, where they are far away from any more favourable area which they could get to in a few hours' march, then an accident of that kind becomes irreparable. For, since once a revolutionary organization is on a war footing it is obviously in no position to keep a check on the enemy's movements or know what information he has, the place chosen for its own first action can only be decided by itself.

The area of Ñancahuazú appeared from the topographical point of view a likely enough guerrilla zone. Flying high above it, or studying a 1:1,000,000 scale map, you see a mountainous region, with deep gorges, and forests as far as the eye can see. The proximity (or at least the geographical appearance of proximity) to the Argentinian border was certainly a powerful attraction to Che, and an advantage not possessed by the other zones under consideration. Thus, in the abstract, or as the crow flies, it was a possible theatre of operations. But it is not the terrain or the geographical situation which make history, but the mass of the people; people live on the ground, in concrete socio-economic conditions which, in turn, determine their relationship to their natural surroundings: population distribution, types of crops and forms of landholding, production relations, class distinctions, the state of communications, the degree of cultural and political homogeneity, and of hierarchical dependence on the traditional authorities – army, Church, civil administration, ruling parties, and so on. Clearly, then, it is not the topography which in the final analysis determines whether or not an area presents conditions favourable to that advanced form of the class struggle which is the armed struggle; it is the presence or absence of sufficiently antagonistic social contradictions.

In any case, there was really no more time to study the natural conditions of the area than the socio-economic ones. There were few animals in the forest; this meant little hunting, and consequently little protein for the guerrillas, and no possibility of building up a store of dried meat. Possibly hunters from near-by villages or even the peasants themselves had decimated the available game. The fact is that the daily job of catching food, which the guerrillas in the central camp took in turns, was always a disappointment. Apart from a few small monkeys in February, one brown bear in March (before Che's return from his exploration of the north,* in which he had suffered seriously from lack of protein, despite the ten or so scrawny birds caught, and the palm-cabbages laboriously dislodged en route), and a few gazelles (*urinas*) flushed out by Ñato, the best hunter

*See Chronology of Che in Bolivia, p. 153.

in the group – the picture was not a bright one. For instance tapirs, the famous *antas*, were never even seen. Consequently the group was soon forced to use up the reserves of food accumulated during previous months, and emerge from hiding to buy foodstuffs from the peasants; each expedition was a security threat, and over a period the fighters became exhausted by carrying supplies on their backs all along the Ñancahuazú, where the ground was hard going and ambushes frequent. The vegetation was thick and often impassable; there were few natural ways through it, so that progress was painful and slow, and it was continually necessary to cut one's way through with a machete; there was also a surprising dearth of fruit trees. The climate was cold and wet in the winter. The waterways were difficult to cross when in spate, and we may remember that a lot of Bolivian guerrillas could not swim – so that the first two men lost were drowned crossing the Río Grande (Benjamín and Víctor).

The Cuban Sierra Maestra was a botanical garden by comparison – compact and small (you could not get lost for more than a day without finding yourself near a house). There was no game but equally no dangerous or harmful animals, and a wealth of fruit trees (mangoes, oranges, pomelos, etc.); there were no insurmountable natural obstacles, plenty of beasts of burden, and because the sea was so close, the climate was healthy and bracing. In itself this difference was not of decisive importance; the same differences would exist as between almost all the mountain chains on the continent and the Sierra Maestra. But what made it decisive was that it determined a certain rural way of life, a certain pattern of social relations. Like many border areas in Bolivia, the Ñancahuazú region combined a wealth of vegetation with a sparseness of population, exuberant natural contrasts with dreary social contradictions. But the difference between the favourable natural conditions of the Sierra Maestra where Che had fought ten years earlier, and the unfavourable conditions of Ñancahuazú would have been merely an irrelevant detail had it not meant that whereas the Sierra Maestra was an inhabited hilly area, socially and economically active, from Ñancahuazú as far as the Río Grande was almost desert land, with what countryside there was socially and economically passive. So much so that in many places the forest was utterly virgin and unexplored; consequently all available maps of the area were full of blank spaces, and of approximations or errors where places were marked; in spots they would show habitations which simply did not exist, thus making it even harder to plan missions, movements of the column as a whole, or meeting places, and making it necessary to spend most of the time exploring the terrain (this would certainly have been equally the case in the Alto Beni or the Chaparo). To develop a 'mass line', it is vital to have at least an approximate knowledge of the material living conditions of the 'masses', their class contradictions, the relations between producers and the traders in the towns, local political traditions, ways and customs, etc. Obviously it would be best not to have to learn this kind of thing from outside, by more or less superficial, academic, abstract methods; better to be able to get to know people as one of them ahead of time, and actually share in their lives. But this requires the presence of guerrillas who, if not themselves natives of the area, at least have some family links with it, for they alone can have all that basic – almost innate – knowledge of the place without which anyone must appear as a stranger and therefore suspect in an isolated and backward area. There were no such men in the group; there was only one Bolivian comrade who spoke a few words of Guaraní, which was the language spoken by most of the Indian *peones* on the *haciendas* along the Paraguayan border. A number of the Bolivians spoke or were learning Quechua and a few Aymará, but these, though indispensable in other places, were useless here. Whether acquired or instinctive, in the manner of sociologists or of *compadres*, only that kind of intimate knowledge of the *specific, local* nature of class exploitation would have made it possible to discover the immediate and concrete, though perhaps unrecognized, needs of the really poor – including the 'regionalist' demands of concern to the population as a whole, which are of overwhelming importance in Bolivia at present (tax exemptions, the reinvestment of petroleum royalties, building roads, municipal credits, election of local authorities, and so on). Without some such kind of minimum programme, a guerrilla group is moving around blindfold; it cannot become part of its surroundings, still less can it recruit local people for its military operations.

Che was fully aware of this. When he unfolded to me his plan for future operations, he asked me to provide him as quickly as possible with an analysis, however rudimentary, of the socio-economic conditions of the peasants in Santa Cruz province. His plan was to move back towards the north, take the village of Samaipata, cross the Cochabamba–Santa Cruz road, and settle in the Santa Cruz area; the first part of this plan was executed perfectly, and the rest would also have been, had not Joaquín got lost for so long with the rearguard. Che knew that an expanding agroindustrial economy (cotton and sugar) such as existed in Santa Cruz would inevitably create an agricultural proletariat, and a fluctuating mass of small landowners having a hard time making ends meet; and it was to that more northern area that he wanted to move, because there the guerrilla force would find very much more favourable conditions for survival and growth than it now enjoyed.

It is perhaps superfluous to point out that the guerrilla group lacked ways and means to approach the masses, because they should have begun at the beginning – and the beginning was the fact that the 'masses' simply were not there. There was so small a population, and what there was was so scattered, that the 'masses' were virtually non-existent. In two weeks' march in the forest, for instance, in February, Che's column only met one family, one peasant, who, as luck would have it, happened to be Honorato Rojas, the man who led the army to the Vado del Yeso, and sold them the entire rearguard. (He was later executed by the ELN.)

The isolation of the various farms was paralleled by the political backwardness of the men working them. Physical isolation goes hand in hand with social indifference. Remember that in the tropical part of the country, the 'peasant problem' is not an 'agrarian problem', in that the endemic hunger for land prevailing in the Indian communities of the Altiplano does not exist there. The agrarian problem in the central parts of the Altiplano and the Cochabamba valley can be formulated in the traditional terms of too many peasants for too little cultivable land, because of land-grabbing by the *latifundistas*. But here the opposite is the case: there is too much cultivable or reclaimable land for too few farmers. The 1952 Agrarian Reform to a large extent drew the teeth of the Indian peasant communities' revolutionary potential by distributing land and thus increasing the numbers of people with the social status of small landowners; but in this area that potential had had its teeth drawn twice over, if one can say such a thing, first because of the superabundance of land, and then because of the rudimentary state of capitalist production relations. Unlike the situation in Santa Cruz, there had not yet occurred here the remoulding of the countryside, and the new spiral of internal social differentiation and class antagonisms that comes with the large-scale exploitation of a concentrated agricultural labour force.

Thus the 'peasant problem', in so far as it existed here, was not the problem of land, or even of land-tenure; it was a whole mass of scattered demands varying from one locality to another (the selling price of produce, cost of transport, profiteering by middlemen, difficulty of getting loans, lack of equipment, etc.). Consequently, the fact that the guerrilla force had no concrete proposals for improving living conditions, which might have caught people's imagination by touching the sensitive points of their immediate social lives, was the fault of local conditions rather than any lack of a basic political programme. (In fact Inti did manage to give some talks to sparse audiences in the few villages the guerrilla column passed through, and this became painfully evident.) A more detailed inquiry would certainly have indicated the danger of such barren local conditions.

I would like however to mention one curious thing – more perhaps than just an anecdote. This area, though ultimately it seemed so unsuitable for the development of a popular war of a guerrilla type, had none the less been the scene of what may be considered the first tottering steps, or perhaps the prelude, of a guerrilla war in the history of present-day popular struggles in Bolivia. For it was here that, at the end of the 1949 civil war, the MNR insurgents, who had been beaten everywhere else in the towns they had tried to capture – and had sometimes succeeded in occupying for a while – found their last refuge before dispersing and reaching Argentina. The MNR militants had even been able to get groups of peasants to rally to the cause of the National Revolution, and it was together with people from the regions of Camiri and Lagunillas, that those who had survived the popular uprising, laid the deadly ambush of Incahuazí, the canyon next to that of the Ñancahuazú, in which so many of the troops of the oligarchy's army perished. The trained members of the MNR, then an underground movement, who had organized that ambush, left from Santa Cruz and Sucre in trucks, and as the survivors of a failed popular revolution, they waged a rearguard battle all the way, though it did not develop into, nor did they even envisage, a guerrilla war properly speaking.

It would thus seem the merest coincidence; but it would have been interesting to have tried to discover traces or memories among the people, and see what lessons might ultimately be drawn from them. Unfortunately, no one in the guerrilla force, as far as I know, at least, knew anything about the episode; indeed I doubt whether many had even heard of the civil war of 1949, a forerunner of the uprising of 9 April 1952, though in its day it made the pillars of the oligarchic regime tremble. Some knew nothing because they were foreigners who knew few details of Bolivian history, and others, though Bolivians, were too young, and had no links with the 'family' of the old *movimientista* school (which, let me say in parentheses, would be comparable to Argentinian Marxist revolutionaries who had no contact at all with any of the ramifications of Peronism).

Why and how did the guerrilla force come to be in this particular part of south-east Bolivia? In the present state of our knowledge it is not easy to give a certain answer to that central question. It was certainly not the area Che himself opted for at the beginning. Once it became clear to him that it was in Bolivia that he was destined to fight as a guerrilla, he centred his attention on the Alto Beni, known as the Yungas area, north west of La Paz. That was why Papi bought a farm there very early on, not far from Caranavi. But it turned out to be very badly situated, near a military camp; a change was considered, perhaps the purchase of a large estate, not far away, but deeper into the *monte*. Che again insisted to Pacho (Captain Alberto Fernández) on the choice of Alto Beni; and he, on arriving in La Paz on 3 September 1966, passed on the order to Papi and Pombo; so clear was it that, as we can see from Pombo's diary, the comrades even considered selling the Ñancahuazú farm which they had bought in the meantime. I myself was told to make as deep as possible a geopolitical study of that area and of the Chapare, north of Cochabamba – a mission I carried out during September under the anxious and suspicious eyes of the Bolivian CP.

Though not absolutely ideal, these two zones, especially the first, did present a combination of favourable conditions. There is no need to dwell on that here. But it is just worth noting that the Alto Beni, in addition to possessing very good natural conditions, was close to the capital, which it provided with grain, vegetables and meat; it was well populated; there was a quite exceptional degree of political awareness for a rural community because, being a fairly recently colonized area, numbers of settlers had come from towns and mining centres, and there were several popular parties with organized cells of militants and supporters; there was also a strong anti-Yankee feeling – though generalized, it was fuelled by the exploitation of the mines by imperialist companies; and so on. I could perhaps best sum all of this up by mentioning that I twice met peasants who lamented the lack of guerrilla preparations in the area, and the failure of their parties to give any kind of lead in that direction. Certainly no agrarian reform in the classic sense would have had any meaning there, either; but a great many farmers, left to themselves by those responsible for the government's settlement plan, lacking technical assistance, and subject to the greed of the wholesalers, middlemen and transport companies upon whom they depended, were so discontented that an armed uprising would soon have found support, and even perhaps fostered the development of a popular takeover of local power.

By the end of October, just before he left for Bolivia, Che received detailed studies of each of these two areas, with supporting documentation (maps, photos, plans etc.); this was not just in topographical and military terms, but first and foremost social and political, including a list of names, hamlet by hamlet, village by village, of sympathizers and possible collaborators. An additional advantage would have been the fact that several Bolivian comrades in the group, Inti and Coco Peredo among others, had been born and raised not far away, on the plains of the Beni, a bit more to the north, below the mountain mass which offered a difficult but natural access to Peru on one side, and the Chapare basin on the other. And, finally, up to that point, the area had been deserted by the army (for instance there was not a single divisional headquarters anywhere near it) and relegated to the background by army intelligence – though the imperialists, more far-sighted and systematic, still kept a lot of feelers out there through their Peace Corps (which sent a written quarterly report to the embassy), a puppet social assistance body directly controlled by them (the Instituto de Colonización y de Desarrollo de Comunidades), and a cohort of 'sociologists' kindly made available by the OAS.

Despite all this, the comrades in La Paz were led during

this time to make a 180-degree change of plan – from the north west of the country to the south east. On 10 September, Pombo had sent a report to Havana, mentioning the purchase by Coco Peredo of a new *hacienda*, south of Santa Cruz, near the Ñancahuazú river, though the Alto Beni farm had not been got rid of. This was because the frequent comings and goings between La Paz and the Alto Beni, combined with my staying in the area, had alerted the Communist Party and aroused their suspicions. It was indeed an area which gave considerable cause for concern: whereas the Party was trying to relieve itself of the burden of the armed struggle by shifting it out of the country, towards the Southern Cone (as was indicated to Monje during 1966, before Che had decided to establish himself in Bolivia in the first place), the choice of this particular zone of operations obviously centred the struggle upon Bolivia. Here is an extract from Pombo's diary, among other passages on the same subject, dated 28 September:

Together with Ricardo [Papi], we are meeting Estanislao [Monje]. We shall be told what questions will be sent to Manila [Cuba] . . .

Estanislao began by stating that what he had promised Leche [Fidel] was to help organize the business of the South, by making four men available to him and handing them over to Mbili [Papi], and in addition coordinating the Brazil affair with Brizola. He said that in the strategic plan the Bolivian affair took second place, and that the organizing and direction of the Bolivian plan were his responsibility, and at the same time that he would be seeking help. He added that these were the promises made in Manila. Then, in reference to the arrival of the Frenchman [Régis Debray], who had for the second time been criticizing the Party, Estanislao says that the Frenchman is closely involved with the Party of Zamora; that in the name of our government he is offering trips here [to Cuba]; that he has visited the Caranaví area; that from here he has arranged a change of situation from the farm to the Alto Beni region, *a sector from which guerrilla fighting could not be shifted to other countries*. He has managed to discover that the central point of the plan is Bolivia and he is abreast of everything that is going on . . .

We told him that we would not accept his arguments, which are opposed to everything we believe. Everything that has happened has been reported back to our country. On top of that, we told Comrade Estanislao two months ago that the plans for the South are now secondary, and that the general headquarters was here because it was thought that this country, at present, offered the best conditions (with which he agreed).

We have decided to leave the district because the farm was within reach of a military post. We think it better to begin finding another place. There are four possibilities: Alto Beni, Yungas, Cochabamba and Santa Cruz. We have agreed to send people to explore these areas. Since the people recruited in Santa Cruz are locals, we shall send them there, with a jeep, etc. At the same time, we are sending the names of the four areas to Manila. We'll decide on one or other in a few days' time . . .

It was in October that the possibility of choosing the Ñancahuazú area became a definite decision. The amount of activity going on around the Alto Beni had made it suspect – not to the military, who were barely aware of it as yet, but to the Party. It was also at this time that relations between the comrades in La Paz and Monje and his colleagues began to deteriorate badly, and Che had given the word to withdraw from too close an association with them. At that time, too, it was discovered that a member of the Bolivian Party secretariat had passed on certain secrets to the Uruguayan Party at their Congress; and this made it seem possible that information might also be leaked in the same way about the choice of a zone of operations. Thus Alto Beni was finally abandoned as the area for the first encampment, and arms and supplies were transported to Ñancahuazú with the object, first and foremost, of putting the Party off the track. That was the explanation given me by Papi himself the following March in the central camp; and it is corroborated by all the documents that have been available since then (including Pombo's diary, which was made public in 1968 by the Bolivian Minister of the Interior).

Paradoxically, however, it seems that this move actually

fitted in with Party tactics; the removal of the theatre of operations also, temporarily at least, removed the threat of forcing its leaders to accept their responsibilities towards the armed struggle at the national level. In this sense, they must have breathed a sigh of relief. But the transfer was even better adapted to Che's own strategy, because it brought him closer to Argentina. That is why he seems to have made no objection when informed of it by La Paz. He had not up to then actually had time to study the information made available by our various researches; nor had he either the personal experience or any basis for comparison whereby to assess the merits of the various areas under consideration. And it is also possible that, in his impatience to return to a guerrilla way of life, convinced as he was of the basic correctness of the way he had chosen, he felt that, if necessary, the adversities of any area could be overcome if tackled methodically. He was absorbed in the work of military training, of selecting people for his guerrilla group and preparing for future contacts, and with all this, he may well have attached only secondary importance to the first placement of the *foco*.

In any case, this last-minute upheaval changed the expected order in which the various guerrilla fronts in Bolivia appeared; the Alto Beni, once seen as the base of the first front, moved into third place, with Chapare becoming the second front and Ñancahuazú the first. The mass of information that had been collected on the first two was left hanging, with no immediate use to put it to. However, it was not wholly in vain, since it later served in the establishment of the second and third fronts. The postponement would not even have been regrettable had research of the same sort been able to be done in the south-east region. But it was not done, or at least not done properly, for lack of time. Consequently the guerrillas had to begin to get to know the features of the area when they were already settled there – and that work of reconnaissance and exploration was still not complete when military operations proper started.

In other words: by the time Che had discovered how totally unsuitable it was as a zone of operations, it was too late to move away and find another, more favourable area – at least without grave risk. That was basically the reason for the setbacks of February and March 1967, and its causes ultimately lay in the planning of September and October 1966.

6

Choice of Time

ÑANCAHUAZÚ was, in consequence of all this, more of a training area than a theatre of operations (though such a distinction is always somewhat artificial). It was certainly in this guise that the guerrilla commanders saw it at the beginning, as is clear from Inti's diary:

Certain journalists and critics of our war have spoken of that camp as though it were the base for regular operations. This is a misapprehension. Ramón [Che] never intended to remain there indefinitely. All the work done there, apart from establishing the underground headquarters, was of the nature I have described: to keep people permanently active, and ensure that they did not lose the habits they had formed.

Che was certainly concerned to preserve discipline and a sense of responsibility in his men by giving them a collective job to do. Like all revolutionaries – perhaps a bit more so– Che was a constructor and an organizer, and any disorder was repugnant to him. Thus he proceeded with methodical care to set up a central camp of a kind which would seem never to have existed before in any Latin American guerrilla enterprise since the days of the Rebel Army. In doing so, he was obviously working and thinking in terms of a long-drawn-out war. In the space of a few months, and in so far as the primitive conditions permitted, he transformed a precarious mobile camp into a real little fortress, spacious and almost comfortable. The careful detail of its material organization was enough to show that what was being created was, if not a fixed operational base, as Inti rightly says, at least a rear base that could fulfil a number of different functions: a military training camp, a political meeting place, a forces' concentration point, a communications centre, an arsenal, a depot for food and supplies and a school for cadres. There was in fact even an outdoor 'class room' where, every day, punctually from 4 to 6 p.m., Che, and the most educated of the Bolivian comrades, El Rubio (Captain Jesús Suárez Gayol, formerly Vice-Minister of the Sugar Industry in Cuba), Alejandro (Commandant Gustavo Machín) and others, gave classes in grammar, political economy, and Bolivian history; and Che added an optional evening class in French. Conversely, some of the Bolivian comrades gave lessons in Quechua.

The advance trenches overlooking the Ñancahuazú river which defended the approaches to the camp, the bread-oven, the field telephone connecting the vanguard with the observation posts, the furnishing and camouflaging of so many caves near by, the planting of an orchard and a well-watered vegetable garden (which would take several months to yield anything), the stocking up of motor fuel for the radio transmitter and receiver (which must suffice until Che could set up the small hydro-electric station he was planning from a near-by mountain torrent), to say nothing of an improvised but far from negligible library – all these things indicate an establishment which, though perhaps not intended to be finally permanent, was certainly more than just provisional. Che had set up something like a general headquarters, and intended to stay there as long as necessary without, it seems, intending to start fighting a moment before time.

This plan, or at least this general attitude, does much to explain the atmosphere of relaxation and freedom from anxiety which prevailed in the camp during his absence in February and March, and the consequent unintentional and unconscious slackening of security measures (with photos, newspapers, notes, and other documents being handed round freely). The discovery of the camp and sub-sequent military mobilization at the end of March did not cause Che to change his view. Had he not had this concept of how the war would develop, many things would seem inexplicable. Why should he have reprimanded Marcos and Antonio so forcefully on his return for their decision to withdraw from the central camp in face of the military offensive, or ordered an immediate counter-march to recover the camp and defend it at all costs? Could it be simply a matter of principle, a step to prevent the group from becoming demoralized and losing its impetus? Why, after the camp had been occupied by the army, who had used deserters as guides, did Che continue working in the surrounding area? He even came back to settle there the moment the enemy left it – coming in almost as they went out.

In any case, it was without doubt the sudden attack by the enemy which transformed this place of training and preparation into a theatre of operations. What had been a rear base was suddenly converted into the front line of a guerrilla war. This change was effected by the initiative of the army, and without the knowledge of the guerrilla leaders who were shocked to hear the news on their return from a journey of exploration. Once the attack had been launched, Che did nothing to stop it – quite the reverse; but he was now, quite unwillingly, forced into a defensive position. Though he then tried to regain control of the operations taking place, the way they had been begun had not been his to choose. That was the price he had to pay for the unexpected extension of his exploratory expedition caused by rivers in spate, the hazards of the terrain and the sheer density of the forest.

First of all, the long period of starvation it involved for all those taking part proved both physically and psychologically taxing for many of the finest fighters, who actually entered their first active combat as virtual invalids; some of the leading cadres, for instance, like Joaquín and Alejandro, got back to camp haggard and worn, their extremities so swollen by oedema that they could hardly bear to wear their boots, and their index fingers almost too large to fit round the triggers of their guns (right to the end, Alejandro, the chief of operations, could never again digest his food properly). More important still, the fact of the exploration's being several weeks longer than planned meant that Che was not present in person at the place and time which turned out to be decisive. The initial cohesion of the guerrilla group and its unity of leadership and purpose were shattered by sheer weight of circumstances. Antonio and the others who were still in the central camp tried in vain to re-establish contact with Che's group; no one knew the area where Che was exploring well enough to go out alone to find him without getting lost, and they had to wait for the arrival of Rolando (San Luis, Captain Eliseo Reyes), a man of outstanding speed and endurance on the march, whom Che had sent as a scout, for contact to be restored.

Che had undoubtedly left orders and plans for emergency action, but there seem to have been no detailed instructions as to how to cope with an attack on the camp or an unforeseen desertion – so unlikely did either possibility appear. Che was never a great talker, even with his closest collaborators, and had certainly kept his ideas about future operations to himself. In any case, these events which seemed at the time fairly minor and innocuous, yet whose repercussions wrought major havoc on the plans that had been prepared, all took place in the absence of the guerrilla commanders; they could not therefore gauge their importance adequately, even in retrospect.

Che realized at once that his vanguard had behaved with extreme imprudence when, desperate from hunger, they appeared with their weapons at the house of a man employed by Yacimientos Petroleros; but he obviously could not have known that the man in question, Epifanio Vargas, was an agent for the Fourth Camiri Division – an informer and guide. Similarly, Che realized at once that the successive desertions of three people from Moisés Guevara's group, one of them a former agent of the Ministry of the Interior, was much to be regretted; but he could not have realized that those obscure figures whose names he did not even know actually knew a great deal about him and the rest of the group. Still less could anyone have suspected that the urban network had by then come under the observation of the American Embassy and the CIA, the latter well established in La Paz where it had been in full control for several months. The Bolivia of 1967, three years after the overt counter-revolution produced by the 'Fourth of November' was very different from the Bolivia Che had known earlier, which had had virtually no system of intelligence or repression. Hence his comparative underestimation of the enemy's ability to infiltrate and get information.

The army was always one step ahead from 15 March onwards, making it impossible for the first core of guerrillas to achieve their potential for consolidation and extension, and more important still, cutting their communications with La Paz. The stages of implantation, exploration and operations, which should in theory have been distinct and successive, were thus run together simultaneously, telescoped in time.

It may seem strange, then, that Che, far from seeing the start of the war as premature or regrettable, threw himself into it with cheerful aggressiveness, as did everyone else. When Coco Peredo suddenly arrived in the camp, out of breath, on the afternoon of 23 March, to announce that a military column had just fallen into the ambush prepared for it in Ñancahuazú, Che, who had been lying reading in his hammock, let fall his book, stood up, and uttered a joyful war-cry. To celebrate, he even went so far as solemnly to light one of the cigars he kept at the bottom of his rucksack for special occasions. To everyone it came as good news, as a relief after a long period of tension and uncertainty. Yet, looking back unemotionally from this distance, it was not at all a propitious moment in the then political situation of Bolivia, for several reasons:

The mass movement was at its lowest ebb all over the country. The repression of workers in May and September 1965 had driven the workers' movement underground, dispersing or destroying its organization, and enforcing a rigid political isolation on the proletariat by depriving it of its natural allies in the universities and among the radicalized petty bourgeoisie. The victorious army, delighted by having its political and social revenge on the MNR, remained united around Barrientos, with as yet no discernible sign of internal dissension. The civilian oligarchy, huddling under the umbrella of the army, fought politely and without any real bitterness over the crumbs of the bureaucratic banquet. In short, nationally, that moment was characterized by relative stabilization as regarded the class struggle.

The guerrilla force had not had enough time to achieve its own political identity, hampered as it was by the ambiguity of its relationship with the Communist Party. That ambiguity was not evident generally or officially when the first operations took place; but Che, who knew that the plenary session of the Central Committee in La Paz at the beginning of January had ratified for the Party the conditions Monje had laid down at Christmas for uniting with the guerrillas, and who also knew of the expulsion of Loyola Guzmán and other members of the urban section of the executive committee of the Young Communists in February, was perfectly clear in his own mind. 'The Bolivian Communist Party is our Enemy Number One', he was heard to say in April; but it saddened him to say it.

However, when the news of the first ambushes broke, it was not in the interest of the CP to publicize their split with the guerrillas. Indeed, they hoped to gain a certain prestige and authority among other sections of the Bolivian left, and it suited them very well for Inti Peredo to appear as a guerrilla leader; through him they could make capital out of the moral profits of the fighting. Everyone knew that Inti was a Party member, but since he held no post of leadership at national level, he could not compromise the Party fully. Like the POR and several other political bodies, the CP even went so far as to publish a communiqué declaring their solidarity; and Kolle, in an interview with a North American journalist, let it be understood that his Party was no stranger to the armed struggle.

This may help to explain why the urban network, as yet underdeveloped and not fully established, hesitated to adopt its own independent political 'personality' and join the mass movement under its own steam, so to say. In all its propagandizing it was heavily dependent on the CP, using their stencils and copying machine, and their offices. (One manifesto in support of the guerrillas, written by the members of the urban network and printed in Oruro, had printed at the bottom of the advertisement: 'Read and pass on *Unidad*' – that being the name of the official Party newspaper – evidently added by the militant who had done the copying.) The handful of activists who made up the leadership of that urban network still thought of themselves as members of the Bolivian Communist Party, and hesitated to claim the right to speak as an independent organization. They did not even know that one such organization already existed, the ELN (founded in the mountains under pressure of events, but lacking any official, date-stamped Deed of Constitution). They had access to no instructions, or programme, or statements of intent which might have provided them with a basis for discussion and negotiation with other political forces. Organizationally, there was as yet no means of communication between the city and the theatre of operations (especially since Tania, who was partly responsible for the rearguard and communications, was with the guerrillas). The members of the urban network had no possibility of making radio transmissions, nor was there any halfway post in Santa Cruz or Cochabamba; the whole group was concentrated in La Paz, far away from Ñancahuazú.

In short, at that date, the urban support system was as yet neither a serious military organization (with allocation of tasks, substitute leaders ready, trained technicians and experience to call on) nor a political organization of any calibre (with a definite political line, channels of internal consultation and the kind of public or mythical 'personality' a revolutionary organization must have, especially if it is operating underground). This embryonic organization, half way between the two, and without any effective leadership, was still too 'political' to function well militarily, and too 'military' to function well politically.

These two characteristics of the *national* situation at that moment – the state of the internal support system, and the general political state of the country – thus contributed to making the guerrilla uprising look like an unexpected and almost unexplained outburst. At the moment of acting, they appeared as a group of insurgents with no clearly defined political position, no name (whether of an individual or of an organization) that could stir the popular imagination or at least enlighten people as to how the origins and purpose of this revolutionary violence related to their own immediate situation.

In this respect, the Bolivian guerrilla force was confronted with an *objective* problem – a problem from outside, from the standpoint of the 'backward' masses rather than the 'enlightened' vanguard. They had suddenly, overnight, to appear on the national scene with which they were not familiar, without having gained admittance and been announced politically, without knowing the password (unlike the landing from the *Granma* which was the culmination of an enormous amount of previous political fighting, mass agitation, and public challenges well recorded in the press: 'This year we shall be free, or we shall die as martyrs.') The same difficulty was to confront the Peruvian guerrillas a year and a half later. So much the same, indeed, that the observations about it made by Héctor Béjar apply equally well to the effects – of surprise, confusion and puzzlement – produced on the nation as a whole by the ambush of 23 March. It came as no surprise to the army, of course, since they already had the fullest information, but it took the masses totally unaware, apart from a few vague rumours in the press earlier in the year. To quote Béjar:

In general we have said that we cannot wait for the subjective conditions necessary to begin the revolution to occur. That is true, but we erred in not waiting to present a justification for starting the guerrilla war, for we needed such justification to be able to give people the basic, objective explanation of our position. Especially since all the people are not, nor will be in the near future, in a position to understand the necessity to revolutionize the system and change it for another, the reasons for starting an uprising must be made abundantly clear.

The reasons for our attitude were ideologically based on an underestimation of the towns: we believed that, should guerrilla fighting break out among the country population, there would be no need to seek to justify it in terms of urban politics which is something totally foreign, far away, and unknown to the peasants.*

In the case of Bolivia in 1967, though there was certainly a similar underestimation of the towns, there were more complex and solid reasons – both logical and personal – for such an attitude.

Implied in the logic of the guerrilla plan was a certain indifference to events – or the absence of events – in the towns. This was because, as we have seen, to seize control of the capital or any other town was not part of its long- or short-term objectives. The time-factor played a significant psychological role in this attitude. With the perspective of an *extended* popular war, and the confidence we all felt that it could be carried on almost indefinitely, there was little incentive for the guerrilla force to make a close study of the details of the immediate situation. Whether the time chosen by fate for the commencement of operations were a little sooner or later mattered little in relation to the expected length of the war being begun. After all, it had to begin some time, even if the first engagement were no more than a skirmish – and what would any of our ambushes look like in five years' time but just that? What was important was that it should continue and develop steadily; and no one thought of the possible connection between the extended war they believed to be desirable and inevitable and the conditions of the moment when it might chance to begin. Since it was going to go on for years, anyhow, what did it matter whether it began today or tomorrow? All the strategy was based on the certainty of that indefinite duration; consequently those first ups and downs were dismissed as mere tactical episodes, of secondary importance, thus obscuring the close interdependence of strategy and tactics, especially in such a precarious situation.

* *Apuntes sobre una experiencia guerrillera*, Lima, 1965.

Then too, in addition to the logic of time, there was the logic of place. The unconcern which the guerrillas certainly showed over what might or might not be happening outside their area and at a non-military level was not, I think, due to attaching too much value to the immediate surroundings of the *foco* and the (virtually non-existent) local peasant class, as was the case in Peru as described by Béjar; it was due rather to seeing the here-and-now struggle in terms of what was, or should be, happening all over the continent. There again, the guerrillas concentrated on the strategic importance of the *Latin American* nature of the expected revolutionary development; this further contributed to their giving only a restricted, non-decisive, strictly local value to the vicissitudes of the Bolivian political game – a game at that time caught up in all sorts of manoeuvrings, compromises and tricks which could have no meaning or interest to anyone who had not grown up in those surroundings. The *total movement of history* tended to conceal the importance of the *immediate local circumstances*, and it occurred to no one to make any kind of link between the dizzying magnificence of the former and the comparative pettiness of the latter. On the continental scale, the scale of the worldwide anti-imperialist struggle, the ups and downs of politicking in La Paz, controlled by the terrorizing forces of the oligarchy, aroused no more interest than any other minor municipal upheaval.

But Che had more personal reasons for feeling as unconcerned as he did. He had emerged from a terribly testing experience – an internationalist battle inside another continent – and it had left him embittered, disappointed and perhaps frustrated. He was longing to hear once again the whistle of bullets, the background music of war which he admitted to having missed for a long time. On foreign soil, the previous year, he had been unable to fulfil himself as a fighter, and he had not as a man felt at home there, historically, culturally or morally. Now, actually in Latin America, he was at last in sight of the key moment of his life, a moment he had been awaiting and preparing for for so long – ever since that distant day after the rebel army had entered Havana, when he told Fidel of his longing to carry on the fight on the mainland, and Fidel had agreed to his doing so. Che's impatience in March 1967 was almost ten years old – ten years of accumulated, and continually delayed, hopes. By joyously ratifying a decision forced upon him by chance, he was responding, no doubt unconsciously, to his own inner need. By openly declaring war on the soil of his own land, he was at last at peace with himself. The joy he felt at coming to grips with the future was the heartfelt joy of embracing his own past. He was opening a new cycle of historical struggle like a man whose life has come full circle. Hence, perhaps, that inner serenity which never left him through all that last campaign, the coolness, detailed, careful and lucid to the point of irony, with which he approached everything that happened. One might call this rather paradoxical attitude an *active fatalism*; there was nothing off-hand or insensitive about it, no sense of being resigned to fate or in any way deluded about it. His attitude was at once tranquillizing and strengthening, the distillation of that ancient wisdom which also underlay the whole of Iberian culture, that ideal which supported the greatest soldiers and philosophers of antiquity, all men of action also given to reflection, men like Scipio, Seneca, Marcus Aurelius and so many others: stoicism. In his personal life as well as his reaction to events, Che had something oddly but definitely stoical about him.

7

The Campaign

WHAT followed is public knowledge. Che's diary, the diaries of the other principal protagonists and the accounts given by the survivors – Inti, Pombo, Benigno – have made the episodes of the actual military campaign into a legend. What still remains shadowy is the painful march of the rearguard of seventeen men under Joaquín, because they were almost totally liquidated by the army. However, two Bolivians who escaped (Eusebio and Chingolo), the written evidence of Braulio's diary, and the statements of the sole survivor of the final ambush (Paco), together make it possible to reconstruct the story.* The day-to-day account of those two exhausting odysseys, as heard from the lips of the survivors and read from the pens of those who took part, depicts an agonizing, day-by-day chain of imponderables, of unforeseeable setbacks and chance events, not the least unfortunate of which was Che's failure to meet up with the rearguard – who were, on 30 August, just before the Vado del Yeso ambush, only a few kilometres from him. The two groups passed within reach of one another and failed to make the contact they had been aiming at for five months. Undoubtedly the campaign met with the most incredible bad luck, but it is not enough just to say so: one must find out just why there was such an accumulation of misfortunes.

What were the conditions that made it possible for the imponderables to determine the issue as they did? In other words: what made all those mischances possible, and how could they be so decisive? Chance, after all, is generally defined as the intersection of two or more necessary chains of events. There must be some general law visible in the way

* See Ernesto González Bermejo, 'La Columna de Joaquín, Odisea en la Selva', *OCLAE Review*, October 1971; 'El Vado de la traición', *Verde Olivo* (Cuba), *Marcha* (Uruguay).

chances occur. It is a postulate of historical materialism that 'the course of history is under the sway of universal internal laws', and this Bolivian campaign, the introductory chapter in the history of contemporary Latin America, is no exception. We can therefore make our own the warning given by Engels:

Here also, on the whole, in spite of the consciously desired aims of all individuals, accident apparently reigns on the surface. That which is willed happens but rarely; in the majority of instances the numerous desired ends cross and conflict with one another, or these ends themselves are from the outset incapable of realization, or the means of attaining them are insufficient. Thus the conflict of innumerable individual wills and individual actions in the domain of history produces a state of affairs similar to that prevailing in the realm of unconscious nature. The ends of the actions are intended, but the results which actually follow from those actions are not intended; or if they do seem to correspond to the end intended, they ultimately have consequences quite other than those intended. Historical events thus appear on the whole to be likewise governed by chance. But where on the surface accident holds sway, there actually it is always governed by inner, hidden laws and it is only a matter of discovering these laws.*

Where should we look to find the 'inner, hidden law' which would enable us to see the successive episodes of this military campaign as its consequences at various stages of time, or indeed to discover the *determining cause* of the major events? It would be wrong to expect to discover that cause by examining the action of the enemy forces, their military effectiveness, their superior fighting strength. It is clear, as Pombo stresses more than once, 'that it was not the enemy forces which caused the temporary defeat of the guerrilla forces'. Indeed the ineptitude of the enemy's forces is positively astounding when one thinks that a tiny handful of men, physically weak in the extreme, lost in hostile terrain and without means of communication, were able to hold out for almost six months against a vast military mobilization, a whole army, supplied by the US with all imaginable

* *Ludwig Feuerbach*, London, 1888.

technical equipment. It was certainly due far more to the outstanding quality of the guerrilla group, than to the mediocrity of the counter-guerrilla forces, that a precarious balance of forces was maintained for so long. Consider: in the field, the ratio of guerrillas to troops was 1 : 100; at the national organizational level, it was 1 : 1,000. Fighters like San Luis, Miguel, Pombo, Benigno or Braulio – to mention but a few – were each worth a whole company of the establishment's regular army.

Though the enemy forces finally won the advantage, it was no thanks to their own activity or their superiority. To be precise, the only thing they had to thank for their ultimate superiority was a handicap which had hampered the guerrilla force from the start. The enemy's military advantage was only made possible by an *internal handicap* in the guerrilla force. We must, then, look to find the determining cause on the side of the guerrillas, in the revolutionary camp itself. We shall find it by looking not at the fighting unit, but at their 'services'; not at the guerrilla vanguard, but at the rear (the communication lines); not at its virtually unbeatable fighting ability, but at its capacity to travel and to obtain food, shelter and medical care. A fighting force needs a certain minimum civilian backing to preserve its fighting strength and keep it going. A guerrilla force must have a support base or it cannot function as a revolutionary lever; cannot, in other words, capitalize on its own power to act. Without a support base, Che's force was obliged to divide into two groups, and each was then inevitably exposed to the danger of deteriorating. In other words, the lack of fixed support bases outside the actual corps of fighters (collaborators, safe channels through which to come and go, guides, sources of supplies and information, and so on) was the fault in the structure, the weakest link of the chain; that was where it snapped, for the enemy had only to put pressure there to break the entire chain. It seems clear to me that the lack of *logistical* support was the hidden determining cause which explains the succession of apparent 'accidents', 'imponderables' and 'mishaps'.

Obviously that lack was not a technical problem, nor one of resources badly administered; it was directly due to a political factor – to the nature of the relationship existing between the guerrillas and the mass of the people. As we have seen, *the guerrillas' political base did not coincide with their theatre of operations*. Where they were actually working there was no political support to speak of. Where there *was* political support, both actual and potential, was in the mines and the cities, and there there were no guerrillas. Thus what was vitally needed was a system of links between the two, to establish and maintain an underground pipeline for bringing reinforcements and provisions of every kind in one direction, and taking back instructions and messengers in the other. But the unexpected opening of hostilities caught most of the link-men inside the guerrilla area and unable to get out (Tania, Chino, Danton, Carlos); and since the theatre of operations was totally cut off from the rest of the country, those who were left outside it were equally unable to get in. All the army had to do to cordon off the area was to block two rather poor roads (from Santa Cruz to Yacuiba, and from Sucre to Camiri). There was nothing watertight or insurmountable about that strategic encirclement of the area; it was by no means impossible to get through, by foiling the Army's system of checking and surveillance which involved first declaring a state of siege and establishing a curfew in the area, and then demanding that everyone show a pass, while they themselves made requisitions and searches along the roads and in the villages. In Venezuela and Guatemala, where the communications network between the capital and the most remote parts of the country is undoubtedly far more complex and active, the army's traditional methods have never prevented the guerrillas' maintaining regular communications with the outside world, or the coming and going of either fighters or collaborators. But there is a reason for that: those lines of communication are kept in being by the civilian population, locally established support networks among the people. They fit into the life of the area for the simple reason that they belong there, and can thus provide the guerrillas with civilian clothes, places to hide, contacts, false papers, vehicles, help in moving both personnel and materials – in other words a basic cover-up that makes it possible to pass or by-pass all the military checkpoints.

Here the guerrillas had no allies of this kind, for no secret or semi-legal political work had ever been done in the area before the fighting began. From the first, the guerrilla force lacked any sure and detailed knowledge of the terrain, of the ways in and out, of local customs – even of the current administrative regulations. They had no local civilian contacts to provide them with this information, and had to learn it the hard way, by bitter experience. They were finally obliged in desperation to resort to sporadic and precarious meetings with peasants chosen at random and to appoint them messengers on the spot. In these circumstances, it was a virtual impossibility for the guerrillas to initiate any outside contacts; no links could be re-established from the inside. Furthermore, Che did not look kindly on the idea of any member of the group's venturing to the city, which to him meant abandoning one's post. (Papi, who was more aware than anyone of the vital importance for the survival of the guerrilla force of contacting and consolidating the 'urban network', knew what Che felt about this and never dared actually to propose himself for such a mission, though he would have been the ideal man.)

The other possibility would have been for contact to be re-established the other way round, from the outside, with the urban network detailing one or more members to go in search of the guerrillas; they could certainly have worked out some kind of cover. But here again there was the problem of the lack of preparation, the fact that the operational area was totally unknown and very far from La Paz, the failure to realize the extreme precariousness of the guerrillas' situation, especially after August, and the absence of any clear orders from a leadership in no position to send directives of any kind. Though there is some justice in laying these failures at the door of the urban network in

La Paz, it must not be forgotten that an intensely centralized organization, in which the leadership is wholly concentrated in the guerrilla *foco* may well, in such conditions
as these, work to the detriment of any capacity for tactical
initiative on the part of the rest of the organization. Undoubtedly the mere presence of Che, for moral and psychological reasons, contributed to inhibiting still further any
decision-making, any initiative which did not receive his
explicit approval. In any case, the police repression soon
resolved the problem by putting the few active members of
the urban network out of action, and thus so discouraging
the others that they either did nothing or went into exile.
So ended the vicious circle of relations – which unfortunately never got further than the psychological stage –
between the rural guerrillas and their urban network, and
also, more generally, their vast rearguard outside the
country: the rearguard was waiting for news of the guerrilla
war before taking any action, while the guerrillas were
expecting the rearguard to give some sign of life, and to send
them reinforcements and messengers.

This absence of local support produced a series of consequences which affected operations considerably:

1. *The theatre of operations had also to fulfil the function of its own
rearguard*

As we have seen, that area did not present the right conditions, either natural or social, for supporting fifty fighting
men for any length of time. Of the two, it was, of course the
social conditions that mattered most: for feeding, housing
and protecting the sick while nursing them back to health;
for supplying the fighters with all their equipment; for
establishing stocks of food and ammunition at various
points; for providing reinforcements and couriers; for carrying food and ammunition from one camp to another, on
mule-back or in rucksacks; for moving past the enemy lines
such heavy material as the later development of the war

would demand; for getting hold of new recruits to replace those fighters lost in battle and, if possible, to swell the numbers. Otherwise, once their stocks of food were used up, and they were forced by their own need or the enemy's pressure to shift their offensive, and to leave their original encampment with its permanent depots of food, fuel, heavy weapons and explosives, how could the guerrillas get more of these things? Neither logistical support, nor reinforcements of men could get in from outside, because all communications had been cut; and they could not come from inside the area, because of hostility, indifference, or the sheer absence of indispensable material resources.

In fact, a support base can be established only where there is an underground political base, and it was just that political base that was lacking. Consequently the guerrilla corps had no one but themselves to rely on for the maintenance of their material living conditions, and the replacement of their fighting equipment. Thus the active fighters became, so to say, their own ordnance corps; the jobs that in wartime (whether it be conventional war or a popular war) normally fall to the rearguard (the civilian population behind the lines in a conventional war, or the popular forces constituting the support base in a popular war), now fell to the military vanguard themselves. The mobile strategic force, the specially trained corps, was thus drawn away from its basic objectives, of attacking, manoeuvring, surprising and destroying the enemy, into tactical tasks which, though of secondary importance as compared with the war, became major and strategic because there was no one else to perform them, no political movement, no surrounding civilian support, no solid rearguard. The combat forces wore themselves out doing non-combatants' jobs. The guerrilla group lost its mobility, being weighed down with all the burdens of coping with the sick, the wounded and the prisoners, which could not be delegated to civilian collaborators. In such conditions, their own physical and moral strength could not but deteriorate; they were slowed down or utterly worn out by a weariness too great for humanity to survive. Each of the Ñancahuazú columns – Joaquín's rear-guard, and Che's centre-vanguard – was its own support base. To the very end the fighters had to bear the burden of servicing themselves.

One example of this combining of jobs was Pombo himself, who was both an indispensable military leader and 'quartermaster general', and had somehow to be two people at once. Finding food, cooking it and transporting it from place to place, thus became almost the prime, relentless, obsessional function of the guerrilla column, absorbing most of its time and all of its members, sometimes turn and turn about, sometimes all at once. In Joaquín's rearguard, especially, given the appalling physical state of its members (apart from Braulio and Negro who were not ill and were both very robust), and the low psychological state of some of them, the search for food rapidly became their dreary, regular, unavoidable central activity. And, as time went on, it became more and more dangerous. In order to eat they had to go near areas where people lived, and those areas were by definition dangerous – being occupied either by the army, or by peasants who were the army's willing or unwilling collaborators. If they did not eat, they would die of hunger; if they went looking for food they would almost certainly be in danger of death from being betrayed to the army or discovered by them. Guerrilla–peasant contact; purchase of food; contact between peasant and the nearest military detachment; detection, pursuit and encirclement of improvised camp with the cooking pot on the fire in the middle; breaking through the encirclement, often at the cost of dead or wounded guerrillas; and a precipitate retreat – until such time as hunger would once again become so unbearable as to start the wretched cycle once again. Such was the pattern of events, each episode following the last one, whereby the rearguard had to twist their way, saved by a hair's breadth each time, until they arrived, on the afternoon of 30 August 1967, at the house of Honorato Rojas, not far from the Vado del Yeso.

2. *The irreparable dispersal of forces*

(a) *The separation from the rearguard on 17 April* was, at the time, a simple accident, a temporary redistribution of forces involving a temporary parting of the ways. Looked at more closely, that 'accident' can be seen as just one more demonstration of the constraints and difficulties which, though not as yet serious, were already hampering the group as a whole without their realizing it. In fact, it was because Tania, Alejandro and Moisés Guevara were ill with high temperatures that they were transferred from the centre to Joaquín's rearguard, with 'El Negro', as doctor, to look after them. To keep them in the centre would have slowed down the march too much at a time when it was important to move forward rapidly and lightly. Caring for the sick placed a heavy burden on the rearguard, but of course there could be no question of leaving them behind. Ordinarily, in an area favourable for guerrilla warfare, there is always a family, a house, a dependable peasant to whom the sick or wounded can be entrusted, together with a doctor, to be hidden and cared for until the guerrillas return to collect them and take them back to join the group, or they are well enough to rejoin the group under their own steam.

But Che knew no one in the neighbourhood, or even within any possible distance, who could be asked for help of that kind, any more than he knew anyone who could act as guide to people wanting to get out, or any house where a halt could be made for more than a couple of hours. Similarly with the four Bolivians who had been refused as recruits; they could not be left in safety (either their own or that of the group) under the surveillance or guarantee of any local collaborator or supporter, and represented a heavy burden as well as a continual risk to the rearguard (and indeed to everyone else too, for two of them deserted later on, in June and July, and led the army to the secret stores buried in caves near the central encampment).

Another factor which made it necessary for the column to divide for a time was the problem of finding enough food for so many people, some of them not active, in any one place. By dispersing somewhat, some of the pressure was removed from the local sources of supply, already decidedly inadequate.

(b) *The final loss of contact* between the two groups brought with it the problem of communications – a problem which was of course inseparable from the problem of the support base.

As it became prolonged, and eventually irreparable, the separation between Che and Joaquín, between the central column and the rearguard, changed its nature: instead of being the mere mishap it was at first, it became an utter disaster whose effects on both were decisive. For four months, the sole objective of each column was to meet up with the other, in order to re-form into a shock force that would have some military value: four months of searching, of fruitless reconnaissance missions. The anxiety and psychological strain were intense because of the exceptional confidence and esteem Che felt for Joaquín, his second-in-command. At times they passed within less than a kilometre of one another without realizing it, because there was no means of communication. The communications problem among scattered guerrilla forces is always a nightmare, at once vitally important and of immense delicacy. It has arisen a lot in Latin America in recent years, when similar misadventures have seriously affected the guerrilla struggle in Venezuela, and Guatemala, and no doubt other places too; but nowhere else has it resulted in such catastrophe.

Che was well aware of the importance of the problem from the first, and hoped if not to resolve it, at least to reduce it, by improving and modernizing his technical communications system. 'Guerrilla warfare must be brought into the electronic era,' he declared to me in March, deploring the uselessness in rough country of the rudimentary walkie-talkies which were all he had for intercommunication among the various sections of the camp, and between the look-out men and the centre. The exploratory march to the north, in February and March, with which so much went wrong because of lack of contact, had highlighted this inadequacy; and such small apparatus as he had got had succumbed sooner than expected to the effects of wear and tear and the weather conditions. That was why, when I was leaving, he asked that, among the people sent to him, there should be an electrical engineer who could repair the old equipment. He also asked for compact two-way radios, weather-resistant, and capable of transmitting to distances of several dozen miles. (Almost all the batteries had run out – there were hardly enough to keep any flashlights going, since of course the transistor radios must always have priority.)

In any case, Che knew that machines can be no more than a temporary and unreliable first-stage substitute for a network of support-points and individual collaborators among the peasants, the dependable human chain of communications which is the only sure and permanent way of resolving the problem of transmitting messages. Indeed all guerrilla experience seems to indicate that the only trustworthy system of communications calls for a thorough knowledge of the terrain on the part of the guerrillas, and a multiplicity of 'letter-boxes' and messengers among the people who live in the area of operations. To be able to settle upon one or more rallying-points over a period of time (say six months) in fact involves having a thorough command of an entire area – guide-marks, the ways in and out, and the distances in real terms, that is to say what the distances marked on the map mean in terms of days' marching, and what kind of vegetation, or climate, or dangers, or obstacles have to be reckoned with. Above all, any exchange of messages between two mobile troops, neither of which knows which way the other is going, demands a fixed stopping place, an intermediate point both groups know and can get to (a hamlet, a safe house, a reliable peasant contact). Usually it is by way of the rearguard that two troops moving separately coordinate their activities, plan their meetings or effect an exchange of positions. In this particular situation, of course, since no one expected the separation to last, no one thought of fixing upon a meeting point for any given date, or of leaving a contact. But had there been a single trustworthy collaborator available in the area, or a single support-point, there can be no doubt that both Che and Joaquín would have thought of making contact by that means.

3. *It was objectively impossible for Che to establish a perimeter of defence in that zone of operations*

The guerrilla force could not dig in in that area and sustain a long-term military siege or break through the enemy's successive moves to encircle it. Though reduced to a strategy of defence, circumstances did not allow the guerrillas to engage in any defensive fighting where they were without exposing themselves to total destruction. With no rearguard to fall back on inside the area, the group could only retreat somewhere outside it, behind the enemy lines. To prevent the gradual erosion of its forces because of the lack of any support base, Che's column was forced to keep continually on the move, hoping to find a support base further north. To do that, they had to break through the army's encirclement and cross the enemy lines. At the beginning of September news of the Vado del Yeso began to percolate through, until it finally became known beyond doubt. From then on, Che knew that there was no one to wait for in the area, and nothing more to be done there. It would be pointless to go back to the south, towards Ñancahuazú, because there would be no support behind him. The only possibility was to move north again, towards Santa Cruz, and find some isolated place where they could rest, leave the sick and incapacitated, recoup their strength, send someone to the city and, in short, draw breath and prepare for the next stage in the struggle. Failing such a haven, he was doomed to roam aimlessly, exhaustingly, with no home base, and with no clearly marked direction. Such unremitting movement, with no halt of any length, involved mounting fatigue, malnutrition and general physical deterioration, in other words a gradual erosion of the group's forces. On 26 September, at Higuera, the death of three outstanding men, Miguel, Coco Peredo and Julio, left the vanguard section leaderless. That particular ambush by the army was strictly speaking the first serious loss suffered by Che's group in its eleven months' existence.

In his diary, Inti Peredo sums up concisely the facts of the situation as it appeared in early October:

The ambush of Higuera marked the beginning of a new and painful period for us. We had lost two men, and had virtually no vanguard left. The doctor was still ill and the column was reduced to only seventeen guerrillas, undernourished because of the prolonged lack of protein, which naturally impaired their capacity to fight. The fate of Joaquín now being known for certain, Che's next steps were directed to looking for another theatre of operations where the terrain would be more favourable. We needed to get in touch with the city at once, to solve our logistical problems and get human reinforcements, for our forces had been eroded and we had not been able to replace the men who had fallen.

Che himself, more laconically, summed up September in these words: 'The most important task was to get away, and look for somewhere more propitious.'

The Vado del Yeso ambush had illuminated the situation abundantly, though disastrously: Che no longer had to keep moving round the area to make contact with a rear-guard; they were all shot dead crossing the Masicuri, half way across the ford, unable to defend themselves because they were carrying their guns above their heads to keep them dry. But Che could not leave Morogoro, the sick doctor, nor Chino, now almost blind and feeling his way, nor those like Benigno who had escaped with wounds from the Higuera ambush. There was no one to leave them with.

To get through the army's tactical encirclement, the column looked for some way out up above, over the tops of the hills. This meant marching at night, because the terrain was completely open. There was little water up there, and provisions were running out: one gourd of water per person per day, and three quarters of a small tin of sardines.

On the morning of 8 October, the sun rose on seventeen guerrillas still on their feet at the bottom of a narrow canyon known as el Yuro. It was freezing cold, clear and sunny. At about ten, Che sent look-out men ahead, who immediately signalled back that there were soldiers barring the way. To go back was impossible, in broad daylight and in open country. The only thing to do was to try to camouflage themselves against the sides of the canyon and wait for nightfall. It was a matter of time. According to Inti, Che reckoned that if they were discovered after 3 p.m. they could resist until dark, and then break through the enemy's line. If they were discovered earlier their chances of resisting long enough were slim. At 1.30, Che sent Aniceto and el Ñato to relieve Pombo and Urbano who were on guard on a slightly overhanging rock. To get to them meant crossing an open piece of flat ground. They were caught by enemy fire half way there, and Aniceto was killed at once. The group had been spotted. The battle had begun too soon.

When darkness fell, the six guerrillas who had been fighting from a position higher up the side of the canyon, almost on a level with the enemy gun emplacements, were able to start moving to get to the agreed meeting point. 'Fernando' was not there.

The true account of the drama then taking place, not far from where the survivors were gathered, suspecting nothing, we may leave to be told by Fidel Castro, in his prologue to Che's diaries. Though he was not an eye-witness, he is the right person to tell the story. For according to the last telegram communiqué sent by Zenteno Anaya, the man directly responsible for the massacre of Higuera, the last words Che murmured before he died were the names of his wife, Aleida, and Fidel.

Afterwards began what was perhaps the most extraordinary exploit of the entire guerrilla war: the breaking out through successive encirclements of Ñato, Pombo, Dario, Benigno, Urbano and Inti, the settlement of the six survivors* in the zone, and their success in leaving the country in a well-organized fashion. Che's guerrilla force, almost posthumously, had fulfilled its basic desire, had come within reach of its goal – a goal which was also its starting-point. They had established roots in the area, be it only on a single acre, in a single family, a single hamlet, an isolated household. Though apparently insignificant, it was this little 'human detail' that made the superhuman odyssey of that escape possible. One is reminded of Archimedes' cry: 'Give me but one firm spot on which to stand and I will move the earth'; that could be the chorus for all the guerrillas in the world, however hopeless things seem to be. 'Give me but one firm spot among the peasants, wholehearted and sincere, however small, and I shall destroy the whole imperialist pack of hounds unleashed against me.' With that 'firm spot', anything was possible: avoiding capture, frustrating the fiercest attacks of the repression, keeping in touch with the city and with the outside world, pausing to rest and gather strength, moving from place to place, advancing.

The way the guerrillas withdrew from the zone of operations with Inti at their head – starting by going back into it – was the first posthumous victory for Che and his comrades in arms. There have been, and will be, many more. For Che was right in forecasting that the war would be long indeed, punctuated by ambushes, defeats, breathing-spaces and new beginnings; with interruptions and variations in the ways and means of fighting, but a steady amassing of strength and experience. The first ten years in Bolivia have been no more than a beginning – a good beginning.

*Originally there were ten men, divided into two groups. The other group of four was liquidated by the Bolivian army at Mizque on 11 November.

8

The Failure to Connect

THE disaster of el Yuro cut short the life of the guerrilla force by decapitating it. Surprised by the enemy at their most vulnerable, with sick and wounded men in tow, in the most unfavourable possible position for fighting (encircled while on the march, in broad daylight, at the bottom of a canyon, exposed to the enemy's gun emplacements, amid open, rocky, land with no kind of vegetation for cover), the small band of seventeen fighters could not, as they had hoped, get north of the Río Grande where they would have been safe and able to recoup their forces. Had they had a bit more time, they would soon have been able to catch their breath and recover their strength. And the guerrilla organization, both as a political plan and an alternative form of national struggle, could have repaired the holes in its fabric which had been caused, almost imperceptibly, by the suddenness with which the fighting had begun, and the rapidity of its development.

We have seen why it was not possible to proceed in an orderly fashion, in other words to await the right political and physical conditions before moving to direct military operations. Arguably, the time could have been made up and the gaps filled as the war proceeded: re-establishing contact with outside; receiving reinforcements of men, food, and medical supplies; developing more widespread and varied political support than it could depend on at the start; catalysing the immense potential for sympathy and dedication which had up to then remained unfulfilled for want both of access to the guerrillas and of adequate political mobilization. But there was no time. Being stopped in mid-action hardened what had up to then been a still fluid situation of weakness; it was as though a snapshot were taken and developed at the worst possible moment, thus presenting a 'still' of an action that might well have developed later in a totally different way. Che's death defined the features of his endeavour for posterity, caught as it were at the awkward age without having reached maturity – its features still unformed, undeveloped. And incorrect though it may be, that is the picture we have been left to try to understand.

To sum the matter up in broad outline: the guerrilla project never had time to find any definite points of entry – human, political and logistical – into the environment within which it was operating. There were no intermediate points which would have established any kind of continuity between Che's long-term project and the means at his disposal in the short term. The absence of such lynch-pins made it very evident from the start what a disproportion there was between a strategy that was in itself impeccable and perfectly coherent, and inadequate or non-existent tactical means hopelessly unequal to that strategy. It was a disproportion which, since it could not be resolved in time, during the course of the action, meant that the strategy itself could only remain at the level of an abstract intention; it could not materialize as it should, step by step, stage by stage, in the given historical reality of Bolivia in 1967. In this sense it is reasonable to suggest that Che's strategy turned out to be too large in relation to the limitations imposed on his tactics; just as Che, the man, was perhaps too large for that particular political and social context.

Things might have been different had he himself intervened only at a more advanced stage as the culmination of an established and developing armed struggle, had there been a basis of earlier achievements upon which to 'continentalize' the launching of a national struggle. As it was, the 'continental' element, because it was present and therefore could not help predominating, to some extent hampered the development of the potentialities of the 'national' element instead of mobilizing them. Clearly, had the initial guerrilla force existed for long enough, it would have been possible to rectify the disproportion between the two elements – national and international, tactical and strategic – by recruiting more people, making local contacts and establishing a support base, and by allowing as much time as was needed to move on from one stage to the next. In so far as geometry can provide us with a useful analogy for understanding history, we may say that the premature beginning and ending of the war have left us with a truncated and distorted (because unfinished) picture of it, like a scalene triangle of which the continental side is too long in relation to the national side, which is in turn too long in relation to the local side (the latter indeed being almost non-existent). Had a suitable theatre of operations been found on the one hand, and more Bolivians been involved on the other, thus reducing internationalist participation to a smaller scale, better adapted to that *initial* stage, the three sides would have formed a well-proportioned isosceles triangle. All the evidence suggests that Che was profoundly aware of the dubiousness of the situation from the first, but that the solution lay not in his hands but, in that initial phase, in those of the Bolivian Communist Party.

This dislocation as between strategy and tactics, end and means, future plans and available tools, affected matters differently at different levels.

1. *At the regional level*: the absence of go-betweens and of any kind of 'associate membership' for local civilians meant that the guerrilla force was, so to say, out of gear with its social surroundings: the vanguard and the mass of the people were there, alongside one another, but without any interpenetration. There was nothing to catch hold of, no way the guerrillas could break into the surrounding society, which had become a solid mass of suspicion or astonishment, smooth and unassailable at any point. Not merely did they not have among them, or with them, a single *natural leader* from the area – and even the most backward region has its natural leaders, by way of whom any stranger must pass in order to be accepted and recognized by the

locals – they had no one from the area at all. In that sort of rural society, social relations are such that the relatives of a guerrilla, his family's friends and acquaintances, their *compadres* and *comadres*, constitute the first foundations of any political support base. In underdeveloped America, the first political alliances of any guerrilla movement are its family alliances – the first and often the last, too, for they are the most secure. It was this that was lacking in Che's case, since the only *camba* members of the group came from as far as the Beni or the Alto Beni. There were plenty of Aymará or Quechua-speaking Bolivians, but unfortunately neither of those languages was spoken here; in this region near Paraguay many of the *peones* spoke Guaraní, which no one in the guerrilla group knew.

In the light of what Che and his comrades had done in the past, it seems legitimate to make a comparison here with their previous Cuban experience. The difference between the Che who landed from the *Granma* in December 1956 in an area unknown to him, and the Che who 'landed' ten years later in the equally unknown and difficult terrain of Ñancahuazú was that in the first case the political organization of the '26 July Movement' had developed throughout Oriente province a network of collaborators, link-men, local stopping-places; these were not in evidence immediately after the landing, because of the imperfect synchronizing of operations, but soon made their presence felt. Here there was no Frank País, no Celia Sánchez, no Guillermo García, no natural local leaders with both an intimate knowledge of the terrain and unquestioned loyalty to the cause.

Certainly, in the long run, what was lacking because the organization had no natural links with the area could have been created by patient political effort. 'The guerrilla is a social reformer,' Che had written, and used often to repeat. 'Social reform' means a local and gradual improvement in the material living conditions of the exploited masses in the area where the guerrillas are working – like the beginnings of agrarian reform which were successful in the Sierra Maestra, and the campaigns for literacy, popular justice and organized medical care. Reforms of this sort presuppose a real grasp of local conditions, both psychological and material. There is no point in bemoaning the absence of a university to illiterate peasants with no primary school to send their children to, or complaining about the lack of roads to families who live in terror of crossing the river when it is in spate because the authorities have not repaired the wooden footbridge for years. Any agenda for reform must begin at the beginning, with people's real and immediate concerns: first build the school, and then suggest the university; first repair the wooden footbridge, and then suggest an asphalt road.

In any case, as we have seen, it was as much the economic and social situation in the area as the guerrillas' lack of knowledge of it which made it impossible to work out any significant policy for 'social reforms'. Even supposing the guerrilla group really had particular reforms to make, or a basic programme of reforms to propose to the scattered peasants and farm-workers, they would have had to become established and settled for some time in one place, and be in a position to supervise the area and its population, in order to do anything effective. Given the state of perpetual motion in which they found themselves, it would have been out of the question. They had therefore to skip the stage of practical reforms and, on the few occasions when they were able to make a personal appearance to the local population, direct their propaganda and speeches straight to the theme of Revolution and the liberation of the continent – an objective so remote as to be virtually meaningless to the peasants of the Masicuri or the Río Grande, who had never met a Yankee in their lives, and did not even know the name of the last president of their own country. Such a revolutionary proposal, put forward by a handful of ragged strangers, could at best have seemed to them no more than an intangible and mystifying vision.

2. *At the national level*: here too the active guerrillas were totally cut off from existing political centres. If we once

again compare it with Cuba ten years earlier, we can see that there the rebel army had its own peculiar external political apparatus, under its control and responsive to its initiatives, but also grafted onto the trunk, so to say, of a massive popular national movement and extending it to a higher level. The core of the Bolivian ELN, cut off among the mountains, was in the precisely opposite position:

It had no such political apparatus of its own, based on a specially worked out programme and responsive to a leadership clearly independent of all other political forces; such apparatus as it had was 'borrowed' from the Bolivian CP as a temporary and precarious measure; its programme had not yet been worked out and understood by the militants; and the distinction between the guerrilla force and the Party's political leadership had so far emerged only in the ambiguity of public policy statements. Furthermore, because of its Communist origins, that external apparatus only had a very small point of contact with the national political situation and its traditionally dominant trends. In other words, there was no Bolivian equivalent – adapted to the specific state of class relations ten years after Cuba – to the 26 July Movement. That movement had grown away as a bold, dissenting branch, from the solid trunk of the orthodox Party, later known as the 'authentic' Party, and became a mass party rooted in Cuban political tradition and broadly based among the people. From its inception, the 26 July Movement was therefore something that grew out of the reality of the national situation. For the Fidel Castro of 1956 – before he had become the unquestionable and unquestioned 'Fidel' of 1958 – Chibás and his movement provided a kind of guarantee to the people, to reinforce the effect of the Moncada episode five years earlier. But in Bolivia the guerrilla force, moving into action unexpectedly before being able to make any public declaration as to its political position, its aims or its real leader, had no such antecedents to depend on.

Amazing though this may seem in retrospect, in view of the international renown it has since acquired, and the objective factors of the time and place, when the guerrilla group made its appearance in March 1967 it was as helpless as a newborn child, and a fatherless one at that, a child for whom no other relative could be found and whose only guardian was the unlikely and unattractive Bolivian CP, which evoked an instant reaction of mistrust. A dangerous position for an orphan. In practice, history, because it is profoundly dialectical, only allows of innovations which develop from an earlier state of affairs, or an earlier stage of social development, already familiar to the mass of the people. Events, ideas, groups, of unknown parentage are, as we know from centuries of experience, rejected as misplaced, unheard-of or suspect Utopias; at most, they are simply left to develop on their own as a kind of baroque curiosity, an undirected venture or a minor sect. It would have been desirable for the guerrilla movement to have appeared *from the first* as the offshoot at a higher level of a national–popular root; it need not have lost any of its originality – in fact it would have been able to establish that originality more firmly. War is the continuation of politics by other means, and politics does not exist in the abstract, but is embodied for every social class in historically defined figures and characteristics, the figures of parties and of leaders, and especially in the case of Bolivia, of populist or trade-unionist leaders.

It goes without saying that in Bolivia, unlike Chile and to a lesser extent Venezuela, where the Communist parties are massive national popular forces, based in the working class and the traditions of the popular struggle, the CP could be no more than a drop in the ocean of the population. This was so for two reasons: first, because it was one party among many in an exceptionally fragmented left, whose rival sectors were remarkably equal in influence, and the only identifiable hegemony was that of the trade-union movement; and second, because it was Communist within a mass movement historically characterized, though to a lesser degree than in neighbouring Argentina, by a specific form of popular nationalism. The Bolivian CP could thus be no more than a source of support, or help, to the guerrillas, necessary perhaps, but as inadequate by itself as any other political group would have been. The guerrilla group must sooner or later draw support from a far broader range of forces, if it was really to be able to get off the ground politically and militarily. Whether committed individually or collectively, officially or unofficially, at the top or at the bottom, bodies like the PRIN, the left MNR, the Marxist–Leninist CP, the young Christian Democrats (a branch of what is now the MIR), the PORs, the independent Marxist groups, all these represented so many sources for recruiting fighters, militants, willing collaborators, sympathizers; similarly with the various trade-union federations which though operating illegally were still in being. All these various bodies, and their leaders, would have behaved very differently had there been a few cadres from each one in the guerrilla force, or represented in it, from the beginning. In them lay the social and political basis for the revolutionary movement on which the guerrillas would sooner or later have to rely.

Isolation and compartmentalization were undoubtedly demanded by the secret and conspiratorial nature the preparations had to have until the venture had reached a certain stage of maturity, but to Che that objective demand responded to a deliberate political concept. That is why all the suggestions I rather hesitantly made at various times that feelers be put out and contacts made outside the narrow limits of the Bolivian CP, so as directly or indirectly to involve other political forces, were firmly and indeed vehemently rejected by the leadership. There was no place for them in Che's view of things. For it was his intention *first* to consolidate and enlarge the guerrillas' own forces, and only *then* get in touch with popular leaders and organized political bodies – on an equal footing, if not avowedly from a position of strength. Here too, the time factor was vital, for it would take the guerrilla group a while to recruit more members and deepen their commitment. For instance, when I spoke of the need to invite a well-known popular leader to the camp (for, not realizing that it was a physical impossibility, everyone believed at the time that the restoration of contact with the 'urban network' was a matter of days, or at most weeks), Che agreed, but said, 'In six months, not before,' because at that point it would have been a bad mistake. That was how Fidel had proceeded in the Sierra: he too was intransigent and 'closed' in the early months, while he was in a position of weakness; but once he had achieved such indestructible military and political weight as to be able to hold his own in an alliance or pact with any sector of the official or established left, however imposing, without compromising the future of the revolution, he became flexible and 'open'. Che had a similar, indeed a heightened, awareness of the snares of opportunism. To make a premature pact with organizations or individuals who, though dedicated, tended to a certain old-style reformism, and whose support could not therefore be considered absolutely dependable and unreserved, would objectively, whatever the intentions of either side in the then unfavourable balance of forces, have been an opportunist error: it would have been sacrificing the long-term interests of the revolution to the short-term interests of the guerrilla war. And there was nothing in his experience of dealing with the leadership of the Bolivian CP to make him change his mind about that.

Everything depended on what 'short term' and 'long term' might mean, and how long a time the guerrilla force would have in which to develop. On 2 December 1957, when Fidel landed on the Playas Coloradas, he was already a national figure, with his own recognized political identity, and there was a political movement secretly supporting him established all over the country. Che's situation was very different. He did not want to make himself known too soon as the leader of the *foco*, intending thus to make it less easily identified, and reduce to the minimum the target for enemy attack. But alas, whereas the enemy's intelligence recognized full well what they were dealing with before the first shot was even fired, the effect on the local people was to make the movement appear as a body without a head, vague and unrecognizable. Hence a vicious circle: the guerrillas could only become consolidated militarily if they received political support, but to get such support they must first be consolidated militarily. With the development of guerrilla action and the work of political mobilization in the surrounding area, the contradiction would probably have been resolved in the course of time. But, tricky though it was, it was a problem which demanded at least the beginnings of a solution at once. All sorts of efforts were made elsewhere to fill these disturbing gaps in the range of political support – especially by Fidel who had more than one personal interview on the subject with influential Bolivians. But there was no time for those efforts to achieve any concrete results. Che himself above all was in no hurry; and at that time no one, either inside the area or out, could have guessed how short a time the guerrillas would have.

One way and another, the guerrilla force was in no state to benefit from, or even mobilize, one hundredth of the capital of popular support that was available and could have been invested at once, before the action started. The number of people who declared after October 1967 that, 'if they had only known', they would have gone into the guerrilla movement blindfold, over the heads of, or if need be, actually against the orders of their party or union leaders, was enormous; even if we divide it by ten, even if we suppose that nine out of ten would not have kept their word, or for some reason or other would not have followed it up, there would still have been enough people to have multiplied the available fighters by ten; and the same is true, *a fortiori*, of the urban rearguard.

Yet all this capital of good will was left untapped. What happened to it? First of all, all these potential cadres, militants or sympathizers had never been informed, either individually or through their leadership, of the nature of the composition of the guerrilla force, or even of the significance of its existence (and there were many who did not know what to think even after operations had commenced, since they received no explanation or reliable information from the guerrillas' urban representatives – who, indeed, had little to give). Then, once events brought them face to face with the truth of the situation, they could find no way of getting in touch with anyone from the central organization. Finally, all these failures to connect meant that the group suffered all the disadvantages of having Che at their head, in terms of the military mobilization of counter-revolutionary forces, without benefiting from the considerable advantages his presence, if announced, could have brought in terms of the political mobilization of revolutionary forces all over the continent.

Che's eruption into the history of Bolivian society – in which he really only came alive after his death – can perhaps best be compared to a delayed-reaction underground nuclear explosion, spreading out in ever widening concentric waves. The rumbling was felt only afterwards in the nerve centres of that society, delayed and to some extent deadened as it was by distance, by the artificial and apparently contradictory mysteries surrounding it, and by the deafening lies and calumny of the enemy's propaganda. The shock, when it came, was none the less shattering, and the surprise traumatic (Teoponte was only one, but perhaps the most painful, sequel in the moral traumatism which affected the petty-bourgeois student class). There is a sense in which Bolivian society has not yet recovered, and the whole of the left still has the 'Ñancahuazú sickness'. In a curious reversal of the normal order, that left – whether revolutionary or reformist, civilian or military, proletarian or nationalist – is still incubating its own guerrilla war, its own form of that extremely healthy 'sickness', now, so long after the first appearance of the symptoms. Just at first, the masses and their representatives could not at once rise to the advanced, radical, well-defined point of view from which the vanguard envisaged the future prospects of their present struggles.

On the other hand, seeing only the vanguard point of view of any total situation does not always allow of adequate reflection on all its objective aspects. The guerrilla *foco* can be likened to a kind of high-pressure revolutionary nucleus concentrated in a remote place, surrounded by a much vaster low-pressure revolutionary atmospheric current. In order to prevent a front of storms and turbulence being produced along the surface of contact by their meeting, time and space were needed in which there could be a natural process of acclimatization and adaptation. However rather than gaining ground horizontally in a gradual process of expansion, the high-pressure *foco* rose vertically like a tornado, appearing suddenly on the people's horizon like a tempestuous column of cloud standing over the far-off forest of the south east. The difference of pressure could not be overcome so soon; inevitably there was a certain shock, a certain stupefaction, in that hidebound, provincial, enclosed society on its first contact with the revolutionary methods and spirit of the guerrillas. From the guerrillas' point of view, for instance, the legitimacy of using revolutionary violence and the importance of Latin American internationalism were taken for granted; these things were part of their lives, they were second nature. But this was because most of them had ten years of revolutionary training behind them; what appeared as an almost unconscious 'second nature' was actually the conscious result of an extraordinary and intense historical experience – the Cuban Revolution. It was something which, without a similar apprenticeship, could not be shared by the Bolivian people as a whole, or even their political vanguards. Indeed both the latter and the former were, unwillingly and unwittingly, affected by the narrow and demagogic chauvinism which is the common inheritance of both the classical style of oligarchic regime and such bourgeois-democratic revolutions as that of 1952.

It was impossible to expect to find in the *beginnings* of a new revolutionary development the forms of consciousness which come as the *result* of ten years of revolutionary development (ten years which could be worth a hundred in terms of lessons taught). It would have been legitimate to expect to find them in the Communist Party, whose ideology and experience went far beyond the narrow terms of reference of the local bourgeoisie; but we have seen what came of that expectation.

In any case, even the vanguard was not immune from variations of revolutionary climate – hardly surprising if one recalls the objective unevenness in the historical background of the different nationalities, and the very varying political education and military experience of individuals. There will normally be misunderstandings between veterans and novices in any group; *a fortiori* there were bound to be certain non-malignant rifts within the central core of guerrillas, especially in the early stages of their existence as a group.

Che never let slip any opportunity, any incident that might have a suitable bearing, to talk to the guerrillas clearly about the whole national problem, outlining the new concept of nationality that was developing out of the experience of the Latin American revolution. He was always very much alive to the complexity of the problem. Indeed his whole life could be said to have borne the imprint of the national problem; it was, in a sense, his own special Calvary. Once, in one of his talks to the group, he recalled how the same signs of irritability had appeared among the Cuban expeditionaries training in Mexico before the *Granma* landing; and it was no mere chance that those who had taken offence at an Argentinian's having been given the leadership of the 26 July Movement were also later the first to desert not only the Movement, but also their own socialist homeland. But Che had also witnessed the care taken by Fidel to restrict the number of foreigners on the expedition, so that the guerrilla group should not become 'a mosaic of nationalities', as he said, when giving his own account of events in a text dedicated to the memory of his Guatemalan friend 'el Patojo'.

Appearances notwithstanding, Che had by no means forgotten that lesson, and endeavoured to take precautions of the same kind for his own 'landing', ten years later. On 27 November 1966, for instance, when only just arrived, he noted in his diary: 'Ricardo has brought some unfortunate news: el Chino is in Bolivia and wants to see me and send twenty men. This involves problems, because we shall be internationalizing the struggle before arranging things with Estanislao.' Clearly, Che was doing his best to slow down the recruitment of non-Bolivians and speed up that of Bolivians – though still submitting to Monje's decisions. This bad news finally turned out to be a false alarm, and the twenty Peruvians were put off for the moment. But the consequence Che feared still came about by other means: he was forced, in spite of himself, to internationalize the struggle simply because he could not get *enough* Bolivian fighters in time. For far worse news was to follow, and this time it was true.

First of all, Moisés Guevara had offered during his first contacts as intermediary to recruit thirty to forty men, the number allowed for in Che's plans. Actually only a quarter of those promised by Moisés ever started out for Ñancahuazú, and of that quarter over half were to prove useless (deserters or unacceptable as recruits). The fact was that Moisés Guevara's organization had been overestimated, though through no error on Che's part: this was the first imponderable and the first disappointment.

Then when the time came, 'Estanislao', instead of contributing to enlarge the forces of the initial *foco*, as planned, set about taking away as many as possible; from inside, he incited those Party militants already in the group to leave it (in late December 1966), and waylaid or dissuaded other candidates from joining it (January–August 1967). To take only one example: some twenty militants and leaders from the Cochabamba local Party decided in August, on their own initiative, to join the guerrillas, whose whereabouts they knew. When the Party leadership got to know about this, a member of the Political Bureau set off at once to Cochabamba to dissuade them, under pain of public and formal expulsion from the Party. The volte-face of the Bolivian CP was thus the second imponderable and the second disappointment.

In sum: what had been hoped for was the coming together and fusion of an armed movement, building itself up and coming forward from within Bolivia (Moisés Guevara had let it be known in 1966 that he was on the point of starting an insurrection with a large number of comrades), and a movement of support and leadership coming from outside. What happened was that the first, internal movement virtually failed to appear at all at the last minute, so that the second, external one was left on its own and in the lurch. The Cuban comrades who had come to officer and support a troop of Bolivian fighters without any experience of guerrilla warfare found that, since they far outnumbered the Bolivians they had themselves to form the troop. This disastrous reversal of the expected proportions resulted, from a strictly technical viewpoint of the effectiveness and distribution of military force, in a terrible waste of skills, resources and fighting abilities. It meant that, despite its profoundly patriotic dedication to national liberation, the struggle looked far more 'international' than was desirable, and the guerrilla force automatically underwent a certain shift of gravity towards the fighters from Cuba.

As we know, that imbalance was worked to death by the political propaganda of the enemy. It was consequently in their best interests to give special publicity to the 'Camiri trial'; and from the first, of all those under arrest, their cameras focussed on me – nicknamed for the occasion an 'International Castroist Agent', and, as ill-luck would have it, not even a Latin American. It was an extremely uncomfortable position to be in, and I had no guidelines as to how best to comport myself in such a situation, for I was placed in a skilfully contrived dilemma: either to behave as in some sense a spokesman for the guerrilla force, and thereby contribute to the enemy's campaign to de-nationalize it ('the Bolivian nation against the Castro–Communist invaders'), or to leave that role to the Bolivians designated as spokesmen, whose responsibility it was, with the concomitant risk that nothing would be said at all, and thereby contribute to the false image the public already had. In any case it was an ideal situation for the psychological manipulations of the CIA and the local armed forces, whose services had been expanded to the utmost for this excellent cause, for which they did everything possible through all the national and international media available to them. It was a terrible time, painful even now to remember. There was a contest to see who could sound the chord of 'patriotism' loudest in stigmatizing the traitorous communist aggression. It became a sick comic opera in which the American Embassy, Military Mission and Police, in their sincere indignation at such a shocking foreign intervention against a sovereign state (yes, a sovereign state), were competing for the leading parts with certain local 'communists' only too anxious to make it clear (especially through such newspapers as *El Pueblo* in Cochabamba) how greatly they too respected the sacred flag of their homeland.

Such a tragi-comedy was nothing new in Bolivia. It had had its première in 1829, when the royalist oligarchy of the young republic of Alto Perú, under the leadership of Dr Olañeta and the banners of the Christian religion, patriotism and the Law, after narrowly failing to murder Marshal Sucre – a Venezuelan by birth, and the victor of Ayacucho – drove him out of La Paz as a foreign invader come to make trouble in the happy homes of this back-yard of the Spanish Empire. Now the oligarchy of *compradores* and dollar-a-line pen-pushers of the independent republic of Bolivia, under the leadership of General Barrientos and the banner of the Christian religion, patriotism and the Law, kindling one another's enthusiasm behind the polished but insecure doors of their presidential Palace, Senate, editorial offices, patriotic and other benevolent clubs, were taking up in chorus the same old song against Comandante Guevara – an Argentinian by birth and the victor of Santa Clara: he was a foreign invader come to make trouble in the happy homes of the back-yard of the Yankee Empire. In 1967, however, that modern empire with its greater resources, made it possible for its servants, the heirs of those masters of the past, actually to make their kill. History repeats itself. But in this instance, Marx's observation does not apply: in this case, the second time it was tragedy too.

9

To Sum Up

THE dialectic never stops: everything has its name, every phenomenon its law. It is not a case of 'science' on one side, tedious and lifeless, bound up in thick volumes which it is the adult's scholastic obligation to read, and on the other the fresh and ever-changing revolutionary war happening now, in which one can snap one's fingers at the discipline of school. History as being made now by human beings is not a day of rest when one can put back into the bookcase History as explained by the founders of historical materialism. Of this Che was well aware. He was both a man who analysed and wrote and a man of action and adventure, and these two 'selves' were totally intertwined. In his own life he put into practice in an exemplary way the tense and contradictory unity of Marxist–Leninism, both as an object of study and a guide to action; he tried it out on himself, one might say, and was ready to undergo whatever rigours it might involve. Now the dialectic of history teaches us that though it is true that phenomena need help from some external cause for their internal contradiction to develop and be resolved, in the final analysis their transformation depends on their own internal cause, in other words, the contradiction within them. Hence, *the external cause can only achieve its effects through the action of the internal cause.*

This seems to me to be the dialectical law which, though it may be stated briefly and sound almost a commonplace, sums up the multitude of accidents, of imponderables, and of piecemeal weaknesses I have had to fit together in an attempt to complete the jigsaw puzzle of Ñancahuazú. Though not always obviously, that law had long governed the history of Latin America – from Cortés to Che, by way of Bolívar. Che was well aware that the restrictions of the dialectic 'of things themselves' cannot be infringed with impunity. He never attempted to break that law, only to make a detour which would bring him back into line with it; and he could do no other, because that detour was forced upon him by the concrete situation in which he was placed. But that 'detour' demanded a certain respite – and it was just that respite that was denied the guerrillas by the surprise attack of the Yuro.

If the guerrilla vanguard, the 'small motor' can be described as the external cause, and the Bolivian mass movement, the 'large motor', as the internal cause, it can be seen that the external cause appeared on the national scene without any immediate or obvious connection with the internal cause – near to it perhaps, but not in the same path, or rather perhaps, parallel but not actually running along the same track. This failure to connect was inevitable, at the beginning. It takes a certain time to get the external and internal causes into true perspective, to get them properly aligned, and in direct contact. The small motor began running before being connected with the large one. To connect up the two, certain historical relationships would have to be re-established, relationships either latent or inadequately understood. Time was short. That period of disconnection, in itself difficult and dangerous, was confronted with full knowledge and understanding by the guerrillas; they got through it by sheer hard work, or more precisely, by will-power – the will-power which Che used to say he had in his own case brought to a fine art.

The initial disconnection appeared in the form of a dislocation in space: there was a hiatus between the guerrillas' zone of operations, near the border and easy to isolate from the rest of the country, and what may be called the historically active part of the country; it was impossible to establish direct contact between the two. Since no such contact could operate from the outside inwards, the guerrillas realized that they must find a different and more favourable area of operations if they were to establish that contact themselves; but they did not succeed in doing so. The physical isolation in space began by submerging the guerrilla *foco* in a vast and deserted area from which there was no escape, and ended by closing in upon the group and swallowing it up altogether, like those gigantic omnivorous flowers that grow in the tropics, which entrap and swallow everything that comes within reach. In this sense, the guerrillas died by being submerged in their own isolation.

But that isolation was itself simply the expression or counterpart of the radical break in the historical patchwork of Bolivian social struggles represented by guerrilla warfare as a method of fighting, or better, perhaps, of its boldly made dialectical 'leap' over a number of squares. Che's revolutionary 'leap' in a relatively backward area, isolated from the more inhabited part of the country, was the transposition into space of a leap forward in time – a leap over the ways of thinking and forms of struggle traditional in Bolivia, at least in recent times.

But there was nothing artificial about that dialectical leap, for in the more distant past it found an authentic echo in the history of the 'War of the *Republiquetas*' just before independence, between 1810 and 1825. The historian Mitre has described the period as 'a story of popular uprisings in the Alto Perú, a war extraordinary in its brilliant fighting, tragic in its bloodthirsty reprisals, and heroic in its quiet and dedicated sacrifices'. Written records of that long war are few and little known, precisely because of its spontaneous and popular character; but *El Diario del Tambor Vargas*, for instance, a journal written on the march by a guerrilla of the time, describes in detail the adventures of a wandering guerrilla group of patriots in the hills, a group in which, alongside the local Indians, there was a curious mixture of Argentinians, Peruvians, Colombians, and here and there a Frenchman or Irishman in search of adventure. Indeed as a method of fighting, guerrilla warfare was a real, though forgotten, part of the Bolivian heritage; but it was a legacy far in the past, with no more recent memories or intermediate links. Rural guerrilla warfare was involved in the birth, or more precisely the gestation, of Bolivian independence: the names of Padilla, Juana Azurduy, Lanza,

Moto Méndez, Lira, Camargo and other popular heroes are deeply imprinted in the national memory. But they are now no more than names, reduced to a kind of sediment in the subsoil of official culture, and thus cannot be compared with the still living and exciting memory of the peasant soldiers of Gómez and Martí in the Cuban consciousness today, or even that of the Argentinian *montoneros* of the last century.

The leap made by the guerrillas, then, appeared to most people as a leap into the unknown; it met with no response in their own experience enabling them to grasp its full implications, received no support from among the existing popular forces, and bore no relation to any of the familiar norms of social behaviour. Hence the predominant reactions of the mass of Bolivians to the guerrilla uprising were incredulity, scepticism or perplexity. And, being destroyed in embryo, the guerrilla group never had a chance of getting closer, of presenting themselves to the people as a visible and tangible alternative in terms of their political options. The guerrillas had no time to make contact with them, nor to convince the masses of the value of this form of fighting – at least before it was too late – nor to get them to see that they could, and indeed must, make a similar leap to the most advanced form of the class struggle – armed insurrection. With no means of influencing the fate of people who themselves had no control over their own fate, Che's guerrilla force sprang up, compact, heroic, legendary and elusive from the first; and the Bolivian people were forced to watch helplessly, spectators by turns fascinated and involved, incredulous and compassionate, of its parabolic career. Only after its destruction did the people grasp that it was their own history that was at issue. And that they will not soon forget.

Everything combined, then, to leave the guerrilla group alone with itself. That solitude was the real war of attrition that wore it down; of that solitude it died. Withdrawn behind distance after distance, it was as though the group wanted to prevent anyone's being there to witness its death;

what no one realized was that each further distance would amplify the echo of the crash, and would endow its grave — which was nowhere and everywhere — with the immensity of a popular legend on a continental scale. What obstacles were placed around it! The solitude of the Vallegrande area, the poorest part of a desperately poor country. The solitude of the little column wandering about in that area of solitude. And amidst all that, the solitude of Che himself in the middle of the encampment, sitting upright on his stool in the evening, by the fire, his khaki felt hat pushed back, drawing slowly on his pipe, and reading perhaps Leon Felipe's poem, *La Gran Aventura*. There he sat, impassible, absent, barely noticing the comings and goings, the bustle, the clatter of cooking pans, the background of swearing and arguments all round him. He remained motionless and distant, like a man transported beyond this world, letting his eyes rest on the flames from time to time with a slight smile, ironic and confident, as though seeing his own inner monologue, as though savouring in advance the unknown satisfaction waiting beyond the horizon in a profusion of glorious struggles.

What is odd is that Ñancahuazú seems ever further away, while Che comes closer. Gradually, as that piece of history is buried in the past and time moves on, as life continues and the struggle is renewed, faithful to itself, the figure of Che stands out more and more clearly; with his quiet step, his gaze, and his clear voice, he seems to remind us of the reality of the war, and to awaken us from the false dream of peace we find so tempting. Che seems to survive his last venture better every day, seeming somehow bigger than his own frustrated plans even though it was the whole of himself that he put into them.

A Political Chronology of Bolivia

16 July 1809   The insurrection of La Paz, and proclamation of Murillo as 'protomartyr' of Bolivian independence, leading to a general uprising all over Alto Perú.

1812–20   Guerrilla war against Spanish royalist forces.

1824   General Sucre, Bolívar's lieutenant, wins the victory of Ayacucho against the Spanish Viceroy.

6 August 1825   Founding of the Republic of Bolivia.

1847–64   Period of the exploitation of *quiña* (quinine).

1864–71   Exploitation of nitre and guano. Melgarejo's presidency.

1879–84   The Pacific War against Chile. Bolivia loses its access to the sea.

1900   The seat of government transferred from Sucre to La Paz.

1933–5   The Chaco War, a disastrous war against Paraguay.

1936–9   The military governments of Generals Toro and Busch, nationalist in character and tending to anti-imperialism.

1941   Birth of the Nationalist Revolutionary Movement (MNR), led by Paz Estenssoro, Siles Suazo and Carlos Montenegro.

July 1946   President Villaroel, an officer sympathetic to the MNR, hanged by the crowd during an uprising in La Paz. Start of a period of reaction.

9 April 1952   A popular uprising. The MNR, supported by the workers, overthrows the oligarchy's armed forces and gives power to Paz Estenssoro. (He had actually been elected President in the 1951 elections, but they were annulled by a military putsch.)

1952–6   The first Paz Estenssoro government. A period of bourgeois-democratic revolution. Universal suffrage restored, giving the vote to illiterate Indian peasants (21 July 1952); nationalization of the tin mines which had up to then belonged to the Patiños, Aramayos and Hochschilds, and were now to be administered by Comibol (The Mining Corporation of Bolivia) (31 October 1952); Agrarian Reform (2 August 1953); establishment of peasant militias in 1964, alongside the existing workers' militias.

1956–60 Siles Suazo's presidency. The armed forces are unobtrusively reconstituted.

1960–64 Second Paz Estenssoro government, with Juan Lechín, leader of the Bolivian Workers' Confederation (COB) and of the left wing of the MNR, as Vice-President. The trend towards the right is accentuated in the economic and political spheres.

1963 Lechín and Paz Estenssoro part company.

21 May 1964 Paz Estenssoro elected again to the presidency, with General René Barrientos as Vice-President.

30 October 1964 Miners' general strike.

4 November 1964 A series of popular riots result in a military *coup d'état*, led by Generals Barrientos and Ovando Candia; Paz Estenssoro forced to flee to Lima.

15 May 1965 Juan Lechín exiled to Paraguay by the military junta. Demonstrations and miners' strikes. A state of siege proclaimed, and mining areas occupied by troops after a bloody repression.

September 1965 Popular uprising in Oruro and La Paz; also put down.

4 July 1966 General Barrientos elected President, with Siles Salinas, leader of the Social Democratic Party, as Vice-President.

September 1966 Miners' strike in the Siglo Veinte and Huanuni mines.

27 November 1966 Signing of the *Pacto campesino-militar* between the armed forces and the official peasant organizations, in the presence of Barrientos and Ovando.

26 January 1967 The death penalty abolished in Bolivia.

1 March 1967 'Guerrillas have been seen in Oriente province.'

8 October 1967 Murder of Comandante Guevara.

20 July 1968 Antonio Arguedas, Minister of the Interior, accused of having sent Che's journal to Cuba. He escapes to Chile. State of siege proclaimed 22 July.

29 July 1968 All parties and political groups move away from a government made up solely of the military.

10 January 1969 Inti Peredo, commandant of the ELN, presents a manifesto declaring that the guerrilla war has begun again.

27 April 1969 General Barrientos dies in a helicopter accident. Siles Salinas becomes President of the Republic.

9 September 1969 Inti Peredo is caught in his hiding-place in La Paz and killed.

26 September 1969 General Ovando takes power, and forms a civil-cum-military government.

17 October 1969 Nationalization of the Gulf Oil Company, carried through under the Minister of the Mines, Marcelo Quiroga Santa-Cruz.

July–October 1970 Failure of an attempt by the ELN under the leadership of Chato Peredo, Inti's brother, to start a new guerrilla *foco* near Teoponte, north east of La Paz.

7 October 1970 Workers' general strike and popular insurrection in La Paz, bringing the progressist government of General Torres to power.

1 May 1971 Opening session of the People's Assembly in La Paz – an organ of 'dual power' consisting of all the elected representatives of the workers, from both the trade unions and the political parties.

23 August 1971 Overthrow of the Torres regime by a fascist *coup d'état*, led by Banzer.

Chronology of Che in Bolivia

15 May 1963 The vanguard of a Peruvian guerrilla column, having come back to Peru from Bolivia, was caught and decimated at Puerto Maldonado (among the dead was the Peruvian poet Javier Heraud). The rest of the column managed to withdraw through the Bolivian forest, and settle in La Paz for two years. Thus the Peruvian ELN was formed, under the leadership of Héctor Béjar and Juan Pablo Chang.

July 1963 The first visit to Bolivia of Jose María Martínez Tamaya, or 'Ricardo', a captain in the Cuban army,* and a close comrade of Comandante Guevara; he travelled under an assumed name, with a Colombian passport.

September 1963– The setting up under Ricardo's aegis of **February 1964** the rearguard of the Argentinian People's Guerrilla Army (EGP) on the Bolivian–Argentine border; it was commanded by Masetti, a friend of Che's, and located in Salta province. Several young Bolivian communist militants were involved: Coco and Inti Peredo, Rodolfo Saldana, Jorge Vásquez Viana, etc.

March 1964 Interview at the Ministry of Industry in Havana between Comandante Guevara and Tamara Bunke, the daughter of German communists who had emigrated to Argentina, and gone back to the GDR after the war. 'Tania', as she was called, received, after a long period of training, Che's first instructions about her mission. She was to get herself accepted in Bolivian high society, and wait to be contacted later.

18 November 1964 Arrival of Tania in La Paz, posing as

---

*The Cuban military hierarchy included three basic ranks: *teniente*, *capitán* and *comandante* – equivalent to lieutenant, captain and major.

Laura Gutiérrez Bauer, an Argentinian. She got her resident's permit in January 1965.

14 March 1965   Return of Che to Havana, after four months' travelling in Africa.

1 April 1965   Che's farewell letter to Fidel, which the latter was to read in public on 3 October, at the presentation by the Central Committee of the Cuban Communist Party.

December 1965   A Cuban revolutionary sent to make contact with Tania in La Paz.

January 1966   Tricontinental Conference in Havana.

March 1966   Arrival in Bolivia of Ricardo from the Congo, via Europe and Cuba (having acquired the further pseudonyms of Papi and Mbili).

July 1966   Arrival in Bolivia of Pombo (Captain Harry Villegas), and Tuma (Lieutenant Carlos Cuello, Che's bodyguard since 1959). A number of Che's companions-in-arms got their nicknames from Swahili, because of their links with the Congo.

July–September 1966   Military training in Cuba of the group of volunteers chosen to accompany him supervised by Che himself. Preparations and first contacts in La Paz. Several meetings between Pombo and Mario Monje, Secretary General of the Bolivian Communist Party. Several of the Peruvian ELN leaders were taking part in the work in La Paz.

September 1966   Arrival in La Paz of Captain Alberto Fernández (Pacho), with instructions from Che as to the location of the area of operations and the choice of political contacts. Régis Debray (Danton or el Francés) set out to explore the Alto Beni and the Chapare, and to investigate the arrangements made in La Paz by Moisés Guevara, leader of a splinter group of the Marxist-Leninist Communist Party (itself set up in April after a split with the Communist Party of Bolivia), who had made it known that he planned to join the armed struggle.

Late September 1966   Stormy interview between Pombo and Mario Monje, the latter definitely alarmed by

Debray's trip, and by the preparations being made. Strained relations with the Bolivian CP.

October 1966   Meeting of the Party's political commission, and preparation of the Ñancahuazú farm with Coco Peredo, Tuma and Ricardo.

4 November 1966   Arrival of Comandante Guevara, via Madrid and São Paulo; he travelled as Adolfo Mena González, an Uruguayan 'special envoy from the OAS'.

Early December 1966   Visit of Mario Monje to Cuba.

31 December 1966   Interview between Che (Ramón) and Monje in the camp at Ñancahuazú. Monje wanted to take over the politico-military leadership of the war, and Che refused. The result was a breach.

8–10 January 1967   A plenum of the Party's Central Committee, meeting in La Paz, ratified Monje's positions.

22 January 1967   'Instructions to Urban Cadres' sent out; the text by Che taken to La Paz by Loyola Guzmán, the network's treasurer.

Late January 1967   Interview between Che and Moisés Guevara.

1 February 1967   Departure of the main body of the guerrilla force (twenty-seven of them – fifteen Cubans and twelve Bolivians) to explore the northern region, towards the Río Grande. This march was intended to take a fortnight, but in fact took six weeks, amid enormous difficulties.

8 February 1967   Crossing of the Río Grande in spate; two people were drowned in this endeavour.

Early February 1967   Arrival at the camp of eight of the expected twenty Bolivians from Moisés Guevara's group.

Late February 1967   The leadership of the Young Communists expelled all members who decided to remain with the nascent guerrilla movement.

6 March 1967   Unforeseen contact by the vanguard of the column led by Marcos (Comandante 'Pinares') with a civilian, Epifanio Vargas, who followed the column back to Ñancahuazú, and made their presence known to the Camiri Fourth Division.

10 March 1967   A military detachment occupied the *casa calamina*, 'the house with the zinc roof', a few miles from the guerrilla camp. The farm, which had remained undetected until then, was the guerrillas' first base of operations.

11 March 1967   Desertion of two Bolivians, who went straight to the military authorities. One of them had worked as an informer for the Ministry of the Interior.

20 March 1967   Che returns to the central camp.

23 March 1967   The first fighting. The guerrillas held off a military offensive in the Ñancahuazú gorges; seven of the army's men were killed, and there was a commandant and a captain among the prisoners.

24 March 1967   Tania's jeep, containing her personal papers, found by the army in a Camiri garage. (Tania, who had brought Ciro Roberto Bustos, Pelado and Debray to the camp in February, was intending to return to La Paz as soon as possible, and get on with her own work there.)

Late March 1967   Four Bolivians from Moisés Guevara's group expelled but, even though disarmed, they had to stay with the guerrillas until further orders.

4 April 1967   The army, guided by the two deserters, found and occupied the central camp. There they discovered an insufficiently buried diary kept by Braulio (Lieutenant Israel Reyes) on the march. Che consequently changed his pseudonym from Ramón to Fernando.

10 April 1967   Successful ambush at Iripiti: ten soldiers killed, two of them officers, and thirty captured by the guerrillas. Death of Rubio (Captain Suarez Gayol, formerly Vice-Minister of the Sugar Industry in Cuba).

17 April 1967   By accident, the rearguard under Joaquín (Commandant Vilo Acuna Núñez), numbering seventeen, one of whom was Tania, lost contact with the rest of the column.

20 April 1967   Arrest in the village of Muyupampa of Ciro Roberto Bustos (Pelado) and Régis Debray (Danton), together with an English journalist, George Andrew

Roth. A Bolivian journalist, chancing to be in the village, took a photograph of the as yet unidentified prisoners in the police yard. That photo, published in *Presencia* a few days later, contradicted the official military statement that the two first-named were dead.

25 April 1967   Death in battle of Rolando (Captain Eliseo Reyes Rodríguez), 'the finest man in the guerrilla force'.

27 April 1967   Arrest of Loro (Jorge Vásquez Viana, a Bolivian), found carrying his weapons, and wounded on a reconnaissance mission. He was taken to Camiri hospital, interviewed by a pseudo-journalist claiming to be a friend, and 'disappeared' from the hospital on 7 May 1967, murdered.

7 May 1967   Juan Lechín, workers' leader and former Vice-President, arrested in the Chilean port of Arica, with a false passport.

Early May 1967   Desertion of Pepe – one of the four rejected Bolivians – from the rearguard.

15 May 1967   In fighting, the rearguard loses Marcos (Comandante Sánchez Díaz) and Víctor (a Bolivian guerrilla).

6 June 1967   Demonstration by the Huanuni Miners' Assembly in solidarity with the guerrillas.

7 June 1967   Declaration by the government of a national state of siege.

10 June 1967   Che, in his search for Joaquín's rearguard, moved north again, towards Santa Cruz, and crossed the Río Grande.

15 June 1967   A state of alert declared by the trade unions.

19 June 1967   The guerrillas reached the village of Morocco; Che set up as a dentist; three military spies disguised as commercial travellers were captured, and later set free; a young peasant recruit, Paulino, from the village, was sent to Cochabamba as a courier to make contact with the urban network, but shortly afterwards captured by the army.

23 June 1967   A new defence pact between miners and

students. The workers declared the mining areas 'free territory'.

24 June 1967 Massacre of St John's Day. The armed forces occupied the major tin mines near Oruro.

26 June 1967 The guerrillas ambushed, as a result of information given by the three soldiers they had released. Tuma was killed.

6 July 1967 The guerrillas occupied the town of Samaipata, on the main road from Cochabamba to Santa Cruz, where they replenished their stocks of food and medical supplies. They then moved on to seek refuge further south, in a virtually impenetrable area.

14 July 1967 A crisis in government: two political parties withdrew from the ruling reactionary coalition. The armed forces in direct control.

20 July 1967 The rearguard in battle near Ticucha, in the Ñancahuazú area; two more of the rejected Bolivians (Eusebio and Chingolo, both very young and with neither political nor military training) deserted.

27 July 1967 Successful ambush mounted by Che's column.

30 July 1967 Three days later, the column taken by surprise in camp, by the army. Ricardo was mortally wounded while covering the retreat.

4 August 1967 The two deserters, arrested soon afterwards, led the army to the 'strategic caves' concealed in the area around the central camp. The evidence found there (photos, notebooks, passports, files, etc.) made it possible for the authorities to disband the urban network (Loyola Guzmán was arrested), and prepare a case for the 'Camiri trial' which had up to then hung fire.

31 August 1967 The Vado del Yeso ambush. Joaquín's rearguard reached the shore of the Río Grande some distance from Masicuri, and were guided by a peasant, Honorato Rojas, towards a ford (*vado*) where a company of infantry of the Manchego regiment – informed a few hours earlier – were waiting in hiding on the riverbank. Seven fighters were killed crossing the river: Joaquín,

Alejandro (Comandante Gustavo Machín), Braulio, Tania, Moisés Guevara, Walter and Polo (Bolivians). Not long afterwards El Negro (Jose Restituto Cagrera Flores, a Peruvian doctor) and Freddy Maimura, were also captured and killed. One survivor, Paco, was taken prisoner. Che heard this on the radio, and abandoned his search for the rearguard. (Honorato Rojas, who betrayed them, was executed by the ELN on 14 July 1969.)

3 September 1967 Skirmish between a squad of guerrillas and a military detachment on the banks of the Masicuri river. Che's column numbered twenty-two. They started returning northwards, in search of a more favourable area.

22 September 1967 The column halted in the village of Alto Seco. In the village school, Che and Inti Peredo appealed to all the local people – their first political meeting. Almost at once, the mayor betrayed their presence to the near-by garrison of Vallegrande.

26 September 1967 With the army on their tail, the guerrilla vanguard were ambushed near the village of Higuera. Coco Peredo, brother of Inti, and a pillar of the underground preparations since 1966, Miguel, leader of the vanguard (Captain Manuel Hernández) and Julio (Mario Gutiérrez Ardaya, a Bolivian university leader) were killed. There remained nineteen men, one wounded (Benigno) and one seriously ill (Moro, a doctor).

28 September 1967 The army captured two deserters from the column, one of whom had left during the fighting, Camba (Orlando Jiménez) and León, the group's cook (Antonio Rodríguez Flores). They were now reduced to seventeen.

Sunday, 8 October 1967 In the Yuro ravine, now far from the Río Grande, the column was located and encircled. Four guerrillas died in the fighting: Antonio (Captain Orlando Pantoja), Pacho (Captain Alberto Fernández), Arturo (Lieutenant René Martínez Tamayo, Ricardo's brother) and Aniceto Reynaga (a Young Communist militant). Three were taken prisoner and murdered: Che Guevara, El Chino (Juan Pablo Chang, a Peruvian) and Willy (Simon Cuba, a Bolivian, formerly a miner in Potosi). The ten survivors were divided into two groups.

12 October 1967   The first group of four survivors was captured where the Mizque flows into the Río Grande, and executed immediately. They were El Moro (Lieutenant Octavio de la Concepción, a Cuban army doctor), Chapaco (Jaime Arana, former Young Communist militant), Eustaquio (Lucien Galván, the group's radio technician, and a Peruvian ELN militant) and Pablito (Francisco Huanca, a young Bolivian peasant).

12 October 1967   The other group of six broke through the tactical encirclement and set out on a long march, pursued hotly by the army and the police.

13 November 1967   El Ñato (Julio Luis Méndez, a Bolivian from a peasant family, formerly a guide in the Peruvian ELN guerrilla column) was killed during an encounter with the army.

December 1967 and January 1968   Inti Peredo and Urbano (Captain Leonardo Tamayo Nunez) arrived in Cochabamba. Preparations were made for the gradual departure from the country of the last survivors: Pombo, Urbano, Benigno (Captain Daniel Alarcón) and the Bolivian Dario.

22 February 1968   Having crossed the Andes on foot, the guerrillas got to the Chilean border, 125 miles south of Arica. The Chilean socialist senator, Salvador Allende, made it his business to welcome them, and went with them as far as Tahiti.

MORE ABOUT PENGUINS
AND PELICANS

Penguinews, which appears every month, contains details of all the new books issued by Penguins as they are published. From time to time it is supplemented by *Penguins in Print*, which is a complete list of all titles available. (There are some five thousand of these.)

A specimen copy of *Penguinews* will be sent to you free on request. For a year's issues (including the complete lists) please send 50p if you live in the British Isles, or 75p if you live elsewhere. Just write to Dept EP, Penguin Books Ltd, Harmondsworth, Middlesex, enclosing a cheque or postal order, and your name will be added to the mailing list.

In the U.S.A.: For a complete list of books available from Penguin in the United States write to Dept CS, Penguin Books Inc., 7110 Ambassador Road, Baltimore, Maryland 21207.

In Canada: For a complete list of books available from Penguin in Canada write to Penguin Books Canada Ltd, 41 Steelcase Road West, Markham, Ontario.